I STILL HAVEN'T FOUND WHAT I'M LOOKING FOR

PAUL WALKER

First published by O Books, 2006
An imprint of John Hunt Publishing Ltd.,
The Bothy, Deershot Lodge, Park Lane, Ropley, Hants, SO24 0BE, UK
office@johnhunt-publishing.com
www.o-books.net

USA and Canada
NBN
custserv@nbnbooks.com
Tel: 1 800 462 6420 Fax: 1 800 338 4550

Australia
Brumby Books
sales@brumbybooks.com
Tel: 61 3 9761 5535 Fax: 61 3 9761 7095

Singapore
STP
davidbuckland@tlp.com.sg
Tel: 65 6276 Fax: 65 6276 7119

South Africa
Alternative Books
altbook@global.co.za
Tel: 27 011 792 7730 Fax: 27 011 972 7787

Text copyright Paul Walker 2006

Design: Stuart Davies Design
davies.stuart@gmail.com

ISBN-13: 978 1 905047 76 5
ISBN-10: 1 905047 76 2

A CIP catalogue record for this book is available from the British Library.

Printed by Maple-Vail, USA

I STILL HAVEN'T FOUND WHAT I'M LOOKING FOR

PAUL WALKER

BOOKS

Winchester, UK
Washington, USA

In memory of

Harry

who taught me so much without saying a word

CONTENTS

PREFACE

Most educated westerners recognise a painful fact: Christianity is finished. Christians often argue that the majority of people still believe in God and that lots of churches, particularly in the third world, are full to overflowing. But for most of us this doesn't wash. Christianity simply doesn't work any more. It no longer makes sense in its own terms and it no longer helps to make sense of the world.

Almost everybody in the West lives near a church, yet young people on the serious quest for meaning and purpose in their lives rarely enter. These people don't for a second think that the Church or Christianity has anything to say in answer to life's searching questions. As a result fewer and fewer people know anything about Christianity; they don't know its basic stories or its underlying myths. According to a recent survey around half of the population in the UK don't even know why Christians celebrate Easter.

For previous generations, the Church was where you went if you wanted to access God, today it seems to be the last place to look. Yet the decline of Christianity has not led to a decline of interest in things spiritual or religious. People have not all become rational atheists. New Age spirituality is springing up everywhere, alternative medicines are more and more popular, Buddhism is growing exponentially and astrologers even write for 'serious' newspapers. People are still searching to make sense of the world, to make sense of their own existence, and seeking to answer for themselves fundamental questions about the purpose of their lives.

Maybe you've concluded that because many Christians believe bollocks then Christianity must be bollocks. The baby has been thrown out with the bathwater. But many of the stories, ideas and doctrines that led Christianity to be the most popular religion in the history of the world still have an immense power. The fact that the eternally relevant teaching of Jesus has been distorted doesn't mean it can't still help you in your own search for meaning.

This book is not intended to make anybody a Christian; it is rather a contribution from the edge, to sketch the possibilities. It's for people who are searching for meaning, for truth, for God. It does not seek to give answers, but rather rejoices in the search. Put it alongside books on Buddhism, meditation, or crystals, as a Christian perspective on the human search to understand what we're doing here.

"I Still Haven't Found What I'm Looking For"

I have climbed highest mountain
I have run through the fields

Only to be with you
Only to be with you

I have run
I have crawled
I have scaled these city walls
These city walls
Only to be with you

But I still haven't found what I'm looking for
But I still haven't found what I'm looking for

I have kissed honey lips
Felt the healing in her fingertips
It burned like fire
This burning desire

I have spoke with the tongue of angels
I have held the hand of a devil
It was warm in the night
I was cold as a stone

But I still haven't found what I'm looking for
But I still haven't found what I'm looking for

I believe in the kingdom come
Then all the colours will bleed into one

Bleed into one
Well yes I'm still running

You broke the bonds and you
Loosed the chains
Carried the cross
Of my shame
Of my shame
You know I believed it

But I still haven't found what I'm looking for
But I still haven't found what I'm looking for
But I still haven't found what I'm looking for
But I still haven't found what I'm looking for...

Lyrics by U2

PART I

IS THERE ANYBODY THERE?

As a human being, one has been endowed with
just enough intelligence to be able to see clearly
how utterly inadequate that intelligence is when
confronted with what exists.

Albert Einstein

Often when I pray I wonder if I am not posting letters
to a non-existent address.

C.S. Lewis

1
PRAYER

I will start with prayer, because that's where we might find some common ground. I doubt if anyone goes through their life without trying it at least once. It may just be when your child or partner is ill or dying, or when you're in desperate straits yourself. It may be along the lines of: "If there's anyone out there, help". It's also been a driving force in my own life, one in which I've come full circle. Learning how we can start to pray, whether we're praying to anything out there or not, is the beginning of our journey.

I first 'became a Christian' 24 years ago. I even joined the Church. I imagined that I was embarking on a lifetime of adventure, a total change of lifestyle. In reality at first the change turned out to be rather limited; it amounted to little more than stopping swearing. Stopping swearing and starting to pray.

Wherever I went in the Christian world I was told of the vital part that prayer should play in the Christian's life. Preachers of every hue said the same kind of things: prayer is the oxygen of faith, without prayer the Christian will never grow. How could a person even begin to consider the divine without talking to God? How could I presume to do the will of God if I never took the time to listen to him? (I still considered God as a "he".) For that surely is the essence of prayer – a two-way conversation with the Almighty. What more privilege could a human being have than to be in contact, in intimate contact, with the maker of the universe? One might imagine it being a privilege to converse with the President of the United States, to meet Elvis Presley or William Shakespeare. But this, let's face it, was the big one. This was personal contact with He who makes everybody else almost irrelevant. At last it seemed as if any search for meaning was over, for the very cause of any meaning was within my grasp. All I had to do was pray. Of course I was told that prayer was not easy, but the rewards were enormous. Some people who prayed displayed an enviable serenity while others were seeing visions and dreaming dreams. I believed the same could happen to me.

And so I moved on. My faith was drawing me deeper and deeper into the life of the Christian community. I was accepted for ordination, I worked as pastoral assistant in the American Cathedral in Paris. I trained at Theological College. I became a priest in the Church of England. After becoming a Curate I planted a church in a housing estate in the north east of England. Lots of people who had never been to church joined and became Christians. I was found by the Times newspaper to be the national Preacher of the Year. I was a recognised expert in mission, advising churches on how to draw more and more people to faith. And all the while at the heart of my own preaching and ministry was the insistence on the centrality of prayer. After all how could I speak about the divine if I never talked to God? How could I do God's will if I never listened to him?

Only – I could never manage it myself.

God knows I tried. My bookshelf groaned with tomes on prayer. I always had a spiritual director to give me fresh and innovative ideas as well as encouraging me to hang on in there. I tried Augustinian prayer, which involved making a biblical passage real to me. I tried Thomistic prayer, which was basically 'prayerful thinking'. I tried Franciscan prayer, imagining God in the natural world. I tried Ignation Prayer, which had me imagining myself in the heart of a biblical passage. I even tried the Swedish method which was not as much fun as it sounds. I sat in silence, I gabbled in tongues. I attended reflective masses and charismatic Bible weeks. They all offered hope but it never lasted. I convinced myself that the problem was me. I was not a good enough Christian. Maybe my preaching was hollow, maybe my ministry was built on straw, maybe I was a typically hypocritical Christian.

Incredibly I even led courses on prayer giving ideas on how to do it. These were always highly successful. It was during one of these that I began to have an inkling that I was not alone. Most of the people who attended such courses were long-standing Christians, whom it appeared still needed help. If such people were so hungry to learn from a person like me how to pray I could only imagine that they were having difficulties themselves. I admitted to such groups that I found prayer difficult, even impossible, but they seemed to take that as an encouragement to try harder. I suspected that they would go away briefly buoyed up with enthusiasm, but be left feeling guilty that they couldn't manage it.

The problem was the unspoken fear of all Christians, a possibility that few like to admit. Whenever I prayed I had the uncanny feeling that I might be talking to myself. How can you really know you're not? Was I clapping with one hand?

If prayer has never been a major part of your life it is hard to imagine what this does to us who believe it to be vital. Perhaps the best thing to imagine is a sexless marriage. I well remember often waking in the middle of the night in a cold sweat because I wasn't praying. I regularly told people of the urgent necessity of prayer, yet I knew myself to be a failure. Of course I shot up a few requests to God, like we all might do, but I never felt that was enough. I wasn't praying with sufficient concentration or dedication. Occasionally I would manage what seemed like a decent amount of effort, but it never worked the next day.

The Church recognised this problem among its clergy centuries ago, so it invented alternatives to praying, cleverly called Morning and Evening Prayer. Because these are called 'prayer' you can pretend that that is what they are, whereas in fact they make you read psalms and passages from the Bible ending with some well-meaning words about 'praying for the people', whatever that means. By continuing to do this I could at least pretend to myself that I was praying but after a few years I gave up even on this, though I never really admitted it.

The fact that I wasn't praying became a constant worry to me. If I was meant to pray and was not doing it, was this doing me serious harm? Would God punish me horribly if I didn't talk to him? At the time my ministry was progressing rather well without my ever needing to pray. My success therefore could not be the result of God's efforts – he never got a look in; apparently any success was down to nothing more than my ego (or worse, could it be the Devil's work?).

I was beginning to come to some awkward conclusions. Whenever I prayed I was coming to God with questions, but he seemed rather rude and never answered them. Of course I persuaded myself that my experiences of life were God's answer, but part of me knew that to be nonsense. I was beginning to think it was all a game to persuade myself that somebody was there; somebody to hear the cry of my heart. But I feared that in reality all my thoughts and cries simply disappeared, nobody heard them because nobody was listening. I was alone. So I prayed less and less. How could I do God's will if he never told me what was on his mind? If prayer was meant to be a two-way conversation, how come I did all the talking? This failure to pray left me feeling guilty and depressed. For years I tried not to think about it.

So eventually I made a life-changing decision. I gave it up. I just stopped praying and stopped trying to pray. I have to say it was a hell of a lot easier than giving up smoking.

It is quite hard to describe what a relief that caused. At first I simply told myself not even to try to pray. I wouldn't allow myself to feel guilty about it. That was harder than it sounds. Yet over time I simply never attempted to speak to God. Whenever I led worship I would say prayers as meaningfully as I could, knowing that for some these were very real, while for myself they were little more than mantras. Whenever others led prayers in my presence I would listen, consider what they were saying, but be quite clear with myself that I was not joining in, in the sense of personally talking to God. I realised I had never really joined in these prayers anyway. In what sense is it prayer to listen to another person talking to God?

The failure to pray as expected had caused an immense amount of guilt. Every Christian talked about prayer, or about meditation or contemplation or quiet times. There always seemed to be the assumption that others were getting something from these times. If I didn't pray I wondered if I could even call myself a Christian. Yet I had never really prayed; the only difference was that I was now being honest with myself. Once I stopped trying to pray the guilt went. And the world didn't fall in. And I was still sometimes successful. And good things still happened. And life still had amazing coincidences. Basically nothing changed except I was not feeling guilty.

Without the overriding experience of guilt, without the nagging feeling that I was meant to be praying at any given moment I was free to consider how to spend my time. For a while I gave my spare moments to the usual entertainments that life offers, and whenever I was alone in silence I would simply let my mind wander. Yet there was something missing. There always had been, with or without prayer.

We live in a strange world in which, if we choose to, we can invade every sense with experiences. We are constantly bombarded with things to watch and listen to. Films, music, the internet can entertain us, educate us, frighten us, amuse us and sexually stimulate us. We come home tired from our busy work lives and allow our senses to be invaded, we rarely give ourselves a moment to rest, just to be, and this can lead to increased exhaustion and stress. If we ever let ourselves just be, if we listen to our own heartbeat and ask ourselves what it is all for, we sense that there is something missing. The churches, the New Age movement and countless other religious and pseudo-religious groups are all aware of how unsatisfied people are with life as it is. And so they offer new ways of prayer, meditation and contemplation. And still people feel frustrated.

The sense that there is something missing in our lives is almost universal. We are alive and we are conscious of ourselves. The very fact of being aware of our existence has made us ask ultimate questions about our lives. This process is sometimes called the 'terror of consciousness', though I prefer to think of it less dramatically as the anxiety of knowing that I exist. Unlike other animals it seems to be part of the human experience to wonder why. It is incredibly difficult to imagine what on earth we are doing here on this planet. The more scientists discover about existence the more terrifying this can become. We can pose our ultimate questions in many ways, but I can imagine nothing better than the title to Paul Gauguin's masterpiece 'Where did we come from, what are we and where are we going?'

Prayer and meditation, whether from a Christian or another perspective, seem to offer a solution to these questions. We somehow resolve them by being in contact with some sense inside ourselves, both the source and the destination of our being, with ultimate reality, whether or not we call that God.

For some people such a practice is clearly valid and life affirming. However for most it is frustrating. The books we read about prayer all seem to be written by experts who have discovered both serenity and purpose in life. Most of us are left feeling inadequate. And should we be surprised? After all, you can buy a fitness video but you will not end up looking like the model prancing around in a leotard!

I fear that a book like this may well end up as another failed attempt to help people. There is a paradox in all of this. We are aware that there is something missing, we sense that it might just be possible to be in contact with that something, yet whenever we try we are left feeling frustrated. I wish I had a simple solution. If I did I would offer my services as a rather expensive guru.

Traditionally prayer is seen as something that can be taught. The problem with this is that we are told that what other people have found helpful is the way to pray. Only for many of us, their way does not help us. Having given up prayer I tried simply to see what happened if I observed my inner thoughts as they occurred. Once I stopped trying to pray I discovered that at the end of each day I find myself reviewing what has happened. In the morning I find myself quietly pondering the day ahead. I run about twenty-five miles a week during which my mind often feels strangely at peace. I have always done such things both before and after I 'became a Christian'. When I gave myself the impossible task of praying I ignored my natural way of being, even suppressed it in the belief that such thoughts were stopping me hearing the voice of God.

My attempts at prayer were probably motivated above all by fear. When I stopped trying, I found that I was still conducting some kind of internal dialogue, naturally. In fact I did find myself thinking, meditating, pondering in silence and when I did I found moments of truth, of spirit and perhaps, dare I say it, of God. I had discovered that I could not ignore my desire to fill the emptiness of my life, but that my being would do this naturally if only I let it. This still demanded effort; it is surprising just how hard it can be to turn off the radio, television or music centre. I just needed to allow myself to be.

And in these moments I have even found myself praying. Not in any attempt to have contact with God imposed on me, but rather for the needs of others. For that is the way of prayer for most people. Children will naturally pray for their families. In the past when I tried to pray, I would attempt to be in contact with God, to think about Him, to be with Him and at the end give Him a list of the needs of others. Now when I say I will pray for somebody I give them my entire attention. I do not pray in the expectation that God will do something for people. It would be morally revolting if he were to ignore the needs of those who were not prayed for. I simply focus above all else on a person's needs. Such prayer has changed my life, because such a focus tends to lead to action. Since I do not believe God will step in and alleviate suffering, I am challenged to ask how I might be able to do it.

This process has taken many years. I have discovered how to pray only by giving up on prayer. The reason for that is that most 'prayer' is an imposition of other people's ideas. We tend to come at prayer with fixed ideas about who we are talking to, what they are like and what we ought to expect from them. From a Christian perspective this means that prayer is talking to the Christian God as revealed in the Bible and so on. This prayer can therefore be rather awkward, because it demands a belief system. Traditional prayer asks that we have certain beliefs about God before we approach Him, and if we find that difficult we might kid ourselves that we cannot pray. The alternative is a kind of internal dialogue with something we don't quite understand but which can still be very real. I sense that many people have this dialogue but don't quite understand it. We might call this 'natural spirituality', which could be described as the basic human response to the anxiety of knowing that we exist.

I cannot help wondering what the effects would be if more people were to give such time and attention to their natural spirituality. For such prayer is not predicated upon belief. When at times in my life I have been desperate I have felt comforted knowing that other people were praying for me. It is the thought that people are giving their time to think about me that can be the most comforting of all. Such thought or prayer could be done as well by an atheist as a Muslim or a Druid. I remember meeting a woman who told me she was going to commit suicide, life was so bad. I told her that I would pray for her. Later, still alive (obviously), she told me that she could not go through with it knowing I was praying for her. My prayers were answered, not by a God who intervened, but by our common humanity. She was overwhelmed to know she was so cared about. Surely, faced with such a situation, even an atheist who has no need of the idea of God can still offer to spend time concentrating on the needs of another human being, even if the word 'prayer' is a problem.

In a wonderful 'Desiderata' Billy Connolly, the comedian, says 'if you don't know how to meditate at least try to spend some time every day just sitting'. And that gets it about right for me, just sitting. I suspect that what our modern world is missing is people who just sit. We have become so over-stimulated by quick fix ideas that we expect easy answers to the most complex problems. Even when faced with the most complex problems of all we want easy solutions: 'give me a way to pray and that'll be alright'. We feel a natural emptiness when faced with ultimate questions and long for there to be a solution. Only there is no solution. But at the same time the questions will not go away. The answer may well lie in accepting the challenge that ultimate questions pose, and living with them. This experience can be called prayer. But if people were simply to sit, to wait and see what happens the results might be way beyond expectations. Such sitting, waiting and listening might actually lead to an experience of God that is not controlled by a human authority – the Church, the Mosque or the Temple.

I do not doubt that traditional prayer works for some and it is what happens when they just sit, but it doesn't work for me. What I am suggesting is not an answer. All I ask is: how many of us take moments in our day just to be? Not to try and talk to God, not to ask ourselves how important we are, or how well we're doing, not to define ourselves by our significant relationships, but simply to be. This is not a forced conversation with a possible other being, it is simply a time to be, in which we might discover what does lie at the heart of our being. Of course the precise way in which we do this will vary enormously, each of us conducts our internal dialogue differently, there is not a 'way'. The moment I start talking about the way to achieve all this is the moment I start imposing my way of prayer on you. And if I were to do that many people would not recognise it as part of their internal dialogue and so would be left as frustrated as with any 'way of prayer'.

Drawing from my own experiences, I believe that it really is that simple. The need to pray is universal; I suspect that it comes from a need to quieten our minds and be open to whatever is within and outside ourselves. Religious authorities have taken this instinct and directed people on what they should be doing with their efforts. Perhaps if those of us who find such an imposition of ideas difficult simply allowed ourselves time to be, however that worked, then we might find our own natural form of prayer.

Of course such a suggestion will never take off. Religious groups could not support it because they do not control it and the rest of the world will have little interest because it won't make any money.

But one of the things that causes so much trouble in the exercise of prayer is the notion of 'God'. We have made this word refer to something so fearful, so powerful that the idea of contact can be extremely difficult. We need to recognise the difficulty that this word, this idea, causes. But we can also recognise that whatever God is, there are only two places where we will meet, and that is inside ourselves and each other. So much for prayer. In the next chapter I want to discuss the object of our prayer.

2
GOD

It rather goes without saying God is a difficult subject. Just for a moment ponder the word – 'God'. What does it conjure up? I am reluctant to presume what your image might be; perhaps it is personal, masculine and powerful. As I grew up my own 'God' was not an old man with a white beard but a well groomed, smart and vaguely frightening figure who looked a little like my Physics teacher (apologies to Mr Wilson!). I cannot remove that picture from my mind. And I guess that every human being is affected by the word 'God' uniquely. If we're honest, each one of us creates God in our own minds, and often in our own image. We all carry our historical and cultural baggage. 'God' means something very different again for Hindus, Muslims, Sikhs or Christians. The theologian Paul Tillich argued that the word 'God' was so loaded that it ought not to be used for a hundred years. I have some sympathy with him, yet as with many words it is hard to think of another: it is the word we have.

I start by talking about the word God quite deliberately, because I have never met this God character.

I used to think I had, but he wasn't real in the sense that my daughter is real. Does this word 'God' relate to any reality at all? Is God an idea we need to help us make sense of the world or is God the ultimate meaning behind the world of which we all occasionally catch a glimpse? If you hope that this book is going to help you answer that question then stop reading now. I have no answer to this question, but I believe it's the most important one we face.

But maybe the answer doesn't matter as much as the question. It is extraordinary how many well educated, well read and intelligent people seem eager to tell me they believe in God. Which when pressed means little more than believing that there is a God. This strikes me as one of the most bizarre ideas humans have come up with. And it works something like this: 'Somewhere or other there is a God, but we can't see Him, hear Him or touch Him so the trick is to be able to believe that He is there despite any evidence to the contrary.' And that in short is how most people I meet think of Christianity.

People seem to think that this belief in this God is absolutely vital. I remember as a teenager telling my grandmother (not a religious woman) that I was an atheist. 'You mustn't say that,' she replied, 'You have to believe in God to go to heaven.' Are we to imagine that this belief really matters that much? That God expects us to be able to think that He exists above all else; that we are to close our eyes to anything that might make us think otherwise, like a nineteenth-century geologist who believes in the literal truth of the Bible? Do we think that God, if there is one, really cares whether we believe He's there or not? Are we really expected to imagine that our eternal destiny depends on such mental gymnastics? There are even hints in some people's thinking that it doesn't really matter how we live or what we do as long as we can make ourselves believe that there is a God.

Questioning the existence of God or gods is relatively new in human history; with a few notable exceptions people in the West didn't doubt the existence of the divine until the Enlightenment in the eighteenth century. The fact is that for centuries the assumption of God was so fundamental that it is impossible to understand the works of great thinkers without it. Literature, ethics, philosophy and even science were all often based on such an assumption. We need to understand this belief to be able to use some of history's great insights.

Yet ironically, for ourselves, now that we live in a world where the existence of God is questionable, it makes us ponder the ideas around God's existence more deeply. When we wonder about God's existence we are forced to ask pretty fundamental questions about life, and there are no simple answers. If you just accept that there is a God, life can seem little more than appeasing, or knowing, or obeying that God. But the alternative, disbelieving in God, can make life seem meaningless, pointless. Atheism can seem as flawed as religion. How, for example, can we be certain that there is no intelligence at the heart of the universe? Do human beings not have a sense of connectedness with each other that can appear mystical? Do not most of us feel that somehow, in a way we can barely describe, there is something more to existence than what we can see, hear and touch? When I think about these things it can seem as if there is a stark choice, God or no God. Maybe it's not that simple. I simply cannot accept that there is nothing more to existence than what I can see, hear and feel, yet I struggle to define what it is. It is at this point that words fail. Almost the moment I try to explain, define or even speak about this I am aware that my words are inadequate. So, with all the qualifications above, I will use the word 'God' as shorthand for the sense of this 'something more' to existence.

Yet can that God be the God of traditional Christian teaching? Here I'm on dangerous ground, for within the Church how we define God is perhaps the most important element of one's faith. Perhaps more people were burnt at the stake for getting this 'wrong' than anything else. (This seems weird, as Jesus didn't spend any time at all persuading people that there was a God or that his God was better than anyone else's.)

Throughout the first few centuries of Christianity it was considered essential that we understood exactly what we meant when we spoke of God. Many councils of worthy Bishops met to define God, to explain Him. For example the Doctrine of the Trinity was worked out, whereby God is one but has three 'persons', the Father, the Son and the Holy Spirit. Each of the three is co-eternal and equal in power and majesty. Much is said in traditional Christian teaching about how the three relate to each other; this is seen as of the very nature of God. The doctrine of the Trinity claims to describe, in some detail, His inner workings. Many Christians would say that believing anything else is wicked heresy. It defines a real Christian from a member of a cult. My only problem is: how on earth do they know? God, we are told, is a deep mystery, and it's impossible to discern the 'Trinity' from reading the Bible. Let's face it, we don't know that much about our own inner workings, let alone those of God.

As a matter of fact I think the Trinity is a very useful metaphor for God who is therefore described as the Father, distant and unknowable (strange image of fatherhood though); as the Son, God who comes to us through humanity; and as the Spirit, God who can be known within our own souls. Only I haven't got the faintest idea whether God is actually like that, and it would be presumptuous of me to say that He was.

In fact the real questions about God are far more fundamental than whether there is an old man who made us and is now watching over us, or exactly what 'He' is like. When people talk about God they are actually talking about the very purpose of existence. It is fairly clear to me that when we consider the fact that we exist and that the universe exists, we have to assume either that it is pure chance or that it has some reason or purpose. If it has reason or purpose, then one of the simplest ways of explaining this is that some higher being or beings have given it that purpose and these have traditionally been called God or gods. Therefore one useful way of thinking about God is as our 'ultimate concern' (Paul Tillich) or as the 'ground of our being' (John Robinson). God becomes less a person and more the very meaning of our existence.

It is probably clear already that I haven't got a clue as to whether there is a God out there or not. Sometimes I wake up and have an almost mystical sense of God. Other times, perhaps faced with the horrors of this world, I assume there can be no such being and that all my beliefs are merely wish-fulfilment. I am an agnostic. Yet whether or not there is a God out there, most of us seem to need Him anyway. For most of us seem to need to give order and meaning to our lives and our existence and one way we do this is to envisage a supreme being. And we give that being attributes which we do not possess, like infinite power and knowledge. But we also give that being attributes that we sense are deeply important like love, mercy, justice and truth. These are attributes we wish for ourselves and we cross our fingers and hope that God has them too.

More than all that; the idea of God carries with it

something very powerful. To illustrate this I will use the example of Jesus of Nazareth. Jesus' message carried terrifying dangers for him because he chose to challenge the assumed order of his day; peasants did not take on the power of the Roman Empire or the Temple in Jerusalem lightly. We know by the fact that he was crucified that Rome did not allow itself to be challenged in this way. Yet Jesus seemed to have an inner strength, a strength that prevented him from having an inflated view of himself or from cringing before those who were preparing to crush him. This strength came from the one he called his father, God.

Many of those who have risked their lives for the sake of something greater have had just such a belief in God. To me two of the great saints of the twentieth century were Mahatma Ghandi and Martin Luther King. Both of these had a trust in something beyond themselves, one as a Hindu, the other a Christian. Both were prepared to risk and face untimely death because of an inner strength which they understood to have come from beyond themselves. This is how I see God. There are simply those who seem to have been given an extraordinary strength that is inexplicable. Of course not all of them are religious, but I suspect most people at times have a deep sense that their strength has come from a source outside of themselves.

And there is a word that describes such an attitude. It is a word that is often completely misunderstood; the word is 'faith'. Faith is something we can have in ideas and in people. The very act of falling in love is an act of faith – for to fall in love is to put your entire being at the mercy of another, knowing that they could break your heart. Fighting for a cause is an act of faith where you put your life at risk for something you think is more important than your life. And in all of these cases faith is stepping into the void, not knowing if there will be anything there to catch you.

Ultimate faith then – divine faith – is to put one's trust in a goodness that lies at the heart of the universe. Such a faith seems to have inspired Jesus and many of his followers since, it inspired Mohammed, the Buddha and countless other great spiritual leaders. It is this faith that is worth preserving; it is this faith that is worth striving for. This is the faith I want.

To labour the point, I began this chapter by indicating that for many people faith is the ability to believe that there is a God. If we extend this we can see that there are many forms of faith that are of this order. The belief that there are UFOs constantly scanning our world, the belief that all illness is physical and that ultimately there can be a medicine which will cure it, the belief that the government knows what it is doing, the belief that Jesus walked on water. All of these kinds of belief have one thing in common; they make the believer feel better. This kind of belief says to people that the world is frightening and unpredictable but that actually it's OK because there is a good God who has it all under control and if only you know it, accept it and believe it you will not feel so isolated and frightened. Looked at like that, the rise of religious fundamentalism should not surprise us, it is almost inevitable in our uncertain world.

The belief system that there is an all-powerful God in control of the universe is often seen as the only one on offer, not only by those who accept it but by those who oppose it. These are the people, described rather poetically by Richard Holloway, the former Bishop of Edinburgh, as the 'cultured despisers of religion'. Such people will tell you that those who hold impossible beliefs are exemplars of faith and then ridicule the idea of faith altogether.

Yet I am convinced that faith has nothing to do with belief. If you are a faithful friend it doesn't simply mean that you believe that your friend exists; if you say you will be faithful to your husband the word is laden with commitment. To have faith is to have a trust that leads to a particular way of living. In relation to God, this faith is more real if it does not involve certainties. Certainty is not faith and it is dangerous; it inspired the bombers on 9/11, it inspires suicide bombers. They know with absolute certainty that God will reward them richly for their sacrifice. Much of the response from the West has been born out of similar certainty. Contrast that with those who have sacrificed themselves for the people of Iraq or

Afghanistan in the belief that what they are doing is right rather than for eternal reward or economic self-interest or revenge. Think of those who have died saving friends, those who have died attempting to ensure a fair distribution of food. These latter people have a belief in justice, goodness and hope but it lacks the hard edge of certainty. To me, it is these people who have genuine and divine faith.

So in all this what is God? I almost get frustrated with myself at this point. It was easier when I thought I understood God, what He was like and what He wanted of me. As I have said part of me has a sense of the divine yet in my mind I cannot be certain what that sense points to. I do not believe that this life is meaningless, and even if it is, I am going to fill my life with meaning and purpose. Furthermore, there have been moments, brief and fleeting when I have woken and felt there is something more to my life, when I have seen eternity in another person's eyes, when my heart has felt strangely serene at an impulsive action which I have done but not understood. In these moments I have sensed a 'more', a presence, a 'something'. This I guess is fairly universal. For others this feeling, this sense, has been much stronger, even palpable. Is this what Moses felt when he walked up the mountain? Is this what Jesus sensed when he went off to be alone and pray? Is this what Mohammed experienced in the cave? Is this what the Buddha sensed under the Bodhi tree? This to me is God.

And it is this presence, this force that at times seems more real to me than virtually anything else, to which I wish to give my life. It may be seen as tenuous, but then surely so are other purposes I might wish to surrender myself to. We give our lives to love and people cheat on us; we give our lives to the pursuit of money and know that it is shallow; we give our lives to the pursuit of fame in order to reassure ourselves that we exist. Perhaps saddest of all, we give our lives to the pursuit of happiness and pleasure and live in a world where depression is becoming an epidemic.

So let us be prepared to postulate an idea – that at the heart of the universe there is something that we vaguely discern but seems to disappear whenever we concentrate on it. This something is a source of love, truth, justice and mercy. This something can give a deep meaning to our lives and help us overcome our own self-centredness and greed. This something leads us into incredible acts of self-sacrifice and drives us on to make the world a fairer place. This something even gives us the idea that perhaps these lives of ours are not all that there is to existence. Does the something exist? What does it matter; for those who have truly sought to serve it have made such a difference that even the idea is sufficient to change the world for the better.

Just such an idea of God seems to have motivated the

founders of all great religions. For many people the old certainties are gone and the genie can never be put back in the bottle. Yet if we throw away all that religion has given us what are we left with? During the twentieth century ideologies seemed to proffer an alternative to religion. Communism was a belief to give one's life to, as was Nazism – neither worked and both led to untold evil. Yet for centuries people had a vision of something, a God who was the source and destination of life and who gave an inner strength to that life as it was lived. Those religions have met a deep psychological need. We may not share the core beliefs of those who founded these religions but I suspect we do share their need.

When I reach such a conclusion I ask myself whether I am alone. I fear that these are the ramblings of an unquiet mind. Yet I also suspect that there must be more people like me, who have this sense of God but find it hard to put into words. Is there harm in people coming together, not to confirm their own beliefs and prejudices but to acknowledge their shared journey and search? I wish to share my life, not with those who have found the answers but those who know how important the questions are.

And I am still troubled by the word 'God'. I am still stuck with all that divine imagery which is both personal and masculine. Surely we cannot even call God personal; and just replacing 'He' with 'She' simply deals with political correctness. Yet to call God 'It' somehow diminishes God – perhaps a whole new pronoun is necessary. Surely God is more than any words could say. It strikes me that the issue is enormous. God remains a mystery; once we say anything at all about God, we limit God. I have hinted at ways in which I feel I have encountered the divine, yet I know that there are many more. Perhaps as many as there are people.

I wish I were more articulate, but I am here dealing with an area about which nobody seems to be able to say exactly what they want to say. For some God is an ever-present reality, for others nothing more than a metaphor and for most 'He' is something in between. I believe that as long as we are not people seeking to defend our own definition of God there must be ways in which we searchers can get together. We come together not to find the answers but to rejoice together in our questions and seek to make the kind of difference to our world that great people of faith have always done.

3
THE PURPOSE
OF LIFE

W hether or not the idea of 'God' is useful, most people at least at some point in their lives ask themselves what the purpose of their existence might be. We wake up in the middle of the night wondering what we're doing and why we're doing it. It's strange that so many people worry about the meaning of life and yet so few talk to each other about it. It seems that we are almost embarrassed about the things that worry us. I referred in Chapter 1 to Gauguin's three questions, 'Where did we come from, what are we and where are we going?' – perhaps these are better summed up in the plaintive cry 'What the hell am I doing here?' There are no easy answers. In fact one of the problems with religion is that it seems to offer ridiculously easy answers. I've often thought that if the answers are that simple, how come the world is so complicated?

It's not only religion that seems to offer easy answers. If you watch any wildlife programme on the TV and witness the life cycle of most animals it is quite simple. The animal survives the perils of infancy, learns how to gather food, finds a mate, reproduces and then carries on eating, reproducing and nurturing its offspring until finally it dies. This is the condition of all animal life. Human beings are animals. It is sobering to consider how much we dress up our existence. We can eat in fancy restaurants but we're still eating, we can surround sexual acts with romance and love but we're still just mating. We can have incredible funeral rituals – but it's still just about dying. Like all animals, survival and sexual reproduction seem to be of overriding importance to the human being.

Yet something in me is disturbed by the idea that eating, sex and bringing up children are the sole purposes of my life. I almost want to scream that there has to be more. What about art, music, literature? What about education? What about love? There has to be a purpose to my life that goes beyond just living and reproducing. Any discussion which involves religion inevitably gets into a philosophical discourse about the nature of existence and the purpose of life and these issues are what have given Christianity its third central tenet – the idea of mission. The fact of the matter is that even if there is no God out there, even if there is no being or essence that can give my life a meaning, I have to create such a purpose to my existence. Yet I do not wish the meaning I give to my life to be simply a self-indulgent way of making me feel better.

Life's meaning seems more than that, both to me and to those I talk to about it. Most people simply take it as a given that lives have an importance beyond survival, and this is one of the reasons we are so moved by lives cut short, or dogged by pain or tragedy.

Traditionally Christianity has called a person's purpose in life their 'mission'. The word has recently been taken on in the business world. The word mission is rooted in a Latin word meaning to send or to be sent. The idea helps to answer that fundamental question 'What am I doing here?' It does this by saying that I am here because I was sent here. I am here to fulfil a purpose and I have been sent to do so by God. I might not understand what God's purpose was in sending me, but it is sufficient simply to believe that God is at the centre of all meaning anyway. The psychological benefit of such a belief is obvious: it gives some sense to the chaos that life can appear to be and I know that many of those who believe they have been so sent have an inner peace. That certainly happened to me when I became convinced that God had called me to a priest. This peace comes from the conviction that one is doing a job that doesn't simply provide material reward but has eternal significance. What we do and how we live actually matters not just to us and those around us but to an infinite God and in all eternity.

Many people reading this will be aware that you don't have to be specifically religious to believe something like this. I have heard many people explain that they have made a decision because they just knew they had to do so, something led them. You do not have to postulate God to have a sense of the other. For example a leading psychiatrist of my acquaintance, who is not a religious man, explained to me that while training in medicine he had an overwhelming sense that he should work in mental health. 'It was quite mystical,' he said. So in a sense his work is fulfilling his mission. This sense that something leads us, something speaks to our inner selves, I would guess is almost universal. The problem often comes when we try to define the source of this 'something'.

Many Christians say that it is God who has led them into their life's 'mission': not only specific Christian ministry but, for example, teaching or going into politics. I always find such practice among Christians to be among their most endearing qualities. The great Victorian social reformers such as Lord Shaftesbury and Elizabeth Fry were motivated by a sense of mission. Even today if you wander down any High Street in Britain you will see a great many charity shops staffed by Christians with a sense of purpose, with a mission. It is Christians who disproportionately staff soup kitchens, homeless hostels and so much more besides. All these people have taken up the idea that their lives have a purpose and interpreted that with a sense of divine calling. Without them our society would be much the poorer.

Only, sadly, that is not all. When many of us think of mission in a Christian context our hearts sink. For in the churches mission has become almost entirely linked to the idea of evangelism. At one time churches provided a great deal of care: they ran the hospitals and mental asylums, they gave food to the poor, they cared for orphans. In the West the Christian Church was the chief provider of welfare until early in the nineteenth century. The problem for churches today is that on the whole they do not need to provide this social support. Given the Salvation Army as an admirable exception, care of the poor, the vulnerable, the unemployed and so on has been taken over by the State, at least in Europe. Churches therefore seek another mission. If churches do not care for the needy they seek another purpose for their own existence. And this appears to be it: having got people to come to church in the first place they tell them that their overriding concern is to get others to come.

So Christians are increasingly defining mission solely in terms of evangelism. That is, sharing the 'good news'. As the churches decline in numbers and influence they have taken it upon themselves to counter this decline with strident efforts at persuading people to become Christians. Churchgoers are encouraged to bring friends to mission events, the 'Alpha Course' invites people to 'explore the meaning of life' when actually they will be told the meaning of life. And despite all such efforts numbers continue to decline.

The Pope declared that the 1990s was to be the 'decade of evangelism'. Amazingly nearly all the Churches agreed. Evangelists and local mission advisers were employed all over; books were printed by the thousand on how to bring people to Christ. I myself was part of this process. Yet despite all that effort and money the decade failed in its primary task. Statistically, for all decades for which we have full records, the 1990s saw the greatest decline in church-going ever recorded in the West. Perhaps the decade of evangelism actually contributed to that decline.

Evangelism cannot be the principal purpose for which we exist. What a strange body that would make the Church. Here is an organisation whose main purpose is to get people to join it, and once they have joined it becomes their duty to get others to join. Other human organisations have a particular primary purpose to which getting new members is secondary. Political parties believe they can better run a country and seek those with similar views to join. Golf clubs exist to play golf and look for golfers to join. Yet a lot of churches behave as if their first task is evangelism, to get people to join – for what?

If you scratch the surface, the main thrust behind evangelism is the belief that a person needs to accept certain things to attain salvation. This runs very deep: whether or not you are religious you probably recognise the idea that your faith is defined by your belief. God, we think, demands that we believe in him. Faith is equated with belief. So the evangelist tries to persuade a person that Jesus was God in person, that he lived a sinless life and that he died to take away the sins of the rest of us. Apparently in order to be forgiven by God you need to believe that this is true. And so you are 'justified by faith'. Firstly, as I argued in Chapter 2, faith is not belief. But secondly and more seriously, as I have already said I wonder why it matters to God what a person believes about events that happened two thousand years ago. Does my eternal salvation really demand that I have to go through mental gymnastics and believe things that are frankly unbelievable? We are told that God is a loving father. What kind of loving father makes his love for his children depend upon whether or not they believe certain things about him? Surely a truly loving parent simply loves and forgives, depending upon nothing. But this seems to be the basis of so much modern-day Christianity. You go to heaven if you have faith, and faith means believing things that are hard to believe. Some even seem to think that God demands that you believe that He made the world in seven days, just as it says in the book of Genesis. Fail to believe that and you're out. Live a wicked life but accept the myth, and at the end you're in.

Most Christians know inside that they do not like evangelism. It is beyond embarrassing to try and persuade somebody to be a Christian. The reason that polite people do not discuss religion or politics is that most people seem to hold dogmatic opinions in both. Some Christians are absolutely certain that their religion is correct, that they are on God's side and everybody else is not, therefore they have a compulsion to convert even if they do not like doing so. After all it must be heartbreaking to see people you love refuse to believe something when you think that such a belief is crucial to salvation, when their bad belief might send them to Hell for ever.

The idea of confusing mission with evangelism stems from the Victorian missionaries who took the message to parts of the world where Christianity did not exist. Africa was a huge success story, in that most of sub-Saharan Africa was converted. Still, today, African churches are massively successful. Forgive me, for I do not wish to be particularly controversial here – but African society is not successful! In fact where Christianity was most effectively imposed in the second half of the second millennium, that is Africa and South America, we see some of the most dysfunctional societies and economies on earth. This is in contrast to Europe where Christianity evolved most slowly, or to North America and Australia where the settlers were already Christian and killed or marginalized the indigenous population, or Asia where Christianity was rejected by the majority.

Success in conversion spurred churches on. Missionaries came back from 'the field' and noticed that a great many people at home were not converted. Chapels and churches were built in vast numbers to accommodate them. Today in England many of those chapels have themselves been converted – to carpet warehouses, blocks of flats and mosques. The attempts at evangelism failed, continue to fail, and still the churches keep trying. Revival, they promise, is just around the corner. Yet in Britain decline has been going on for the last 150 years. It is one area at which we lead America. But even in the US signs of decline are everywhere, especially among the young.

Pushing people to 'do mission,' to 'be evangelists,' fulfils that basic urge with which I began this chapter. Question: 'Why am I here?' Answer: 'To bring people to a living faith.' This is an all-consuming purpose and for those who believe it is their calling it can be very satisfying. I speak from experience. For many years I saw that as my duty, to bring people to faith. In order to fulfil this calling, I moved to Sunderland in the North East of England and began a church from scratch. Within a year we had over sixty people attending worship, most of whom had never been to church before. Over time many became Christians. It was and remains one of the most satisfying periods of my life. But it was while there that I began to question this role. What was most valuable in that church was not what people believed but what they did. That church enabled neighbours to get to know each other, it began organising community events. Ultimately it played a part in drawing the community together. I suspect that few of those who attended the church believed what I wanted them to believe – it was the sense of community that was transformative, not belief.

If the Church has ever had a valuable role it has been in making a difference to society, not in what it encouraged people to believe. Karl Marx for example referred to this in his comment that 'Religion is the opiate of the masses'. What I think he meant was that in encouraging poor people to believe that their suffering would end in heaven they were stopped from trying to change their condition. In Victorian England a belief in rich rewards in heaven became a means of social control. A similar belief, in the wonders of paradise, seems to have been a motivating factor for the suicide bombers on September 11th. Yet at their best churches have played a part in transforming society far more effectively than Marxists. Today in Britain for example Christian Aid has the slogan 'We believe in life before death' urging action rather than belief; the organisation seeks to give material aid to the poor of the third world rather than converting them.

The secular world has reclaimed the word mission. Mission statements, though now somewhat passé, are written to describe the ultimate purpose of any organisation or business. When we see a friend walking with intent we might say 'You look like a woman with a mission' - again we are referring to their sense of purpose.

If we seek to achieve something single-mindedly and with all our strength it is similarly called a mission.

And life can seem pretty empty if it has no purpose. We have a word for it: it is pointless. The Christian concept of mission still remains one of the best concepts for helping us deal with the apparent pointlessness of existence. Because having a mission in life can make life itself fulfilling. On the whole people find the most self-fulfilment when they are absorbed in something that gives their life a purpose. Most satisfaction seems to come when that purpose involves helping others, like the great Victorian social reformers mentioned earlier in this chapter.

On the whole people seem most content with their lives when pursuing some purpose beyond narrow hedonism. Almost invariably when I learn about somebody who has died in preparation for a funeral the qualities that are most valued are those of generosity, kindness and selflessness, 'he always put others before himself.' Likewise, in helping people to overcome depression, one of the most powerful tools is to help them think beyond themselves, to how they might be able to help others.

There seems to be deep within the human psyche a need to help, to give, to share. When this need is translated into action it produces a sense of well-being and purposefulness in the person who acts. Though we might begin with a sense of duty, in helping others we find, as a by-product, that this gives us a wonderful sense of fulfilment. We cannot afford to lose this sense of duty that leads to altruism and care either for our society or for each other. We may not believe that God is telling us to do something specific, but many of us do have an almost mystical sense that we ought to pursue particular paths. This is our mission, to make a world a better place; to build what Jesus called 'the Kingdom of God' where the first shall be last and the last first. What better purpose could any life have? This is far beyond simply persuading people to believe things. This can give our lives the very meaning that they so often seem to lack. This is the mission that an open-minded faith can still offer the world.

We are not here long; in geological terms, merely the twinkling of an eye. We live at best 80 or 90 years; we seek to fill those years as best we can. Something within us tells us that we matter and that we're meant to be here. It can be very hard to explain; we can be so lost for words that we hardly discuss it, but we want to know what our destiny might be.

In the first two chapters I talked about the idea of the 'other', of God being something almost intangible yet oddly real. This notion is of the same order as our striving for meaning. They are related. For if God is our 'ultimate concern' then the idea of God can also give us our ultimate purpose. This is not idle speculation. There can be few more contented people than those who can look at themselves in a mirror and believe that they are doing what they should be doing.

PART II

MYTH, MAGIC, SIGN AND SYMBOL

Sir, I have found you an argument; but I am not obliged
to find you an understanding.
Samuel Johnson

There is always a well-known solution to every
human problem – neat, plausible and wrong.
H.L.Mencken

4

THE BIBLE

My favourite broadcast programme, in any medium, is on British Radio. It has been around since the 1940s and is a kind of conversation called Desert Island Discs. On the programme some famous, worthy individual is interviewed on the premise that they have been shipwrecked on a desert island and have for company a wind-up gramophone and eight records as well as a book and a luxury item. The programme is basically an explanation of their choices of music (I have chosen mine for when I get invited!). When it comes to the book, they're told that they already have a copy of the Bible and the complete works of Shakespeare, so they have to choose something else. I can only guess that this stems from the 1940s when it was presumed that unless these works were already there they would automatically be chosen by too many people. Today, when told that the Bible is already there many guests seem to snort, as if they would never consider reading it in the first place. What a tragedy. But Christians have only themselves to blame.

What springs into the mind when we think of the Bible - religious instruction classes in school or church? Adam and Eve versus Darwin? The Ten Commandments? Miracles? Even if you've never actually read anything in the Bible the likelihood is that a word that will spring into your mind and that is 'boring'. Considering the Bible remains the world's best seller; that most people have quite easy access to it; that page for page and word for word it retails very cheaply; it is incredible how few people have actually read much of it. I include in this church-going Christians and those who call themselves Bible believers, who may have heard passages read in church but have rarely sat down to read the book itself.

Traditionally the Bible is seen as one of the principle ways in which God communicates with the world. It is often called 'God's word'. I once read in a religious tract: "If you want to understand life read 'the maker's manual'." Utter nonsense. But before I continue, a warning. I have an agenda, and it is this. If you have never read any of the Bible I hope that by the end of this chapter I might have persuaded you to do so. I want ordinary, intelligent people like you to know something about this incredible book. Don't just leave it to those who read it as if it is the word of God handed down.

The Bible is a library of books written over a considerable period of time. I realise that for Jewish people the Hebrew Scriptures are what constitutes the

Bible. This Christians traditionally call the 'Old Testament'. The Christian scriptures were written some time later by the followers of Jesus of Nazareth and Christians call these the 'New Testament'. For the purposes of this chapter I am effectively treating these books as one, and for short hand I am calling the traditional sixty-six books that Protestants accept as canonical 'The Bible'. I do not intend thereby to offend those whose Bible is slightly or considerably different.

However we think of the Bible, one of the major reasons that so few people read it is because of the way most Christians present it. At some level most Christians invest the Bible with a greater authority than any other book. At the most extreme there are those who believe that the books of the Bible were effectively dictated by God and that every word is literally, scientifically and historically true. For others the Bible might contain factual errors about, say, science or history, but it is nevertheless a book inspired by God and therefore has divine authority. This makes rational consideration of the Bible difficult, often impossible. When Christians open that Bible they assume that they are reading the word of God. After reading it in many churches the reader will say something like 'This is the word of the Lord'. So the words of the Bible are right simply because they are in the Bible. It can be very hard for Christians to understand just how difficult other people find this belief.

Those who think that the scriptures have divine authority find immense comfort in their belief. It means that the eternal God has spoken to humanity and we can read and understand what he wants to say to us. On occasion the results of such beliefs border on the comic where, for example, we have the faintly ridiculous sight of archaeologists searching for the remains of Noah's Ark in the mountains of Turkey, convinced that it must be there because the Bible tells them it is. Likewise, however much evidence is shown for Darwin's theory of evolution, there are those who simply refuse to accept it. Evolution must be wrong because the Bible says the earth was created by God in seven days a few thousand years ago. The reason people believe this is not because creation 'scientists' have found a little evidence, but that the Bible itself is seen as the ultimate science textbook. 'Why,' the argument goes, 'try and find out how the world got here when the maker himself has told us?'

Most scientists do not engage in arguing about such issues because the arguments themselves are not scientific. Those who disagree with this approach do not simply ignore Christians, they also do not read their book. The Bible itself has become a problem because of the way some Christians read it. This is true of all books that are considered divinely inspired. Few non-Muslims have read the Koran, and even fewer non-Mormons have read the Book of Mormon.

Of course many Christians are embarrassed by the kind of arguments expressed by those who call themselves Bible-believers or fundamentalists. But even these Christians will enter into the most detailed discussion of, for example, whether the Bible permits women to have authority in society, whether homosexuals can practice and whether divorce might be permitted in certain circumstances. Outside their immediate circle they are ignored. Most people have concluded that women have equal rights to men despite what the Bible says. The equality of the sexes has been one of the greatest improvements in western society in the last century. The vast majority of people simply accept this as a fact, they do not want women to be subject to their husbands and therefore when they read these words in the Bible, they dismiss them.

I was recently invited to join the ethics committee of the Psychology department of my local University. Ethics is a fascinating subject and one that Christians find very challenging. This is so because they believe the essentials of all ethical questions are in this ancient manuscript. Even when I had a higher view of the authority of scripture than I do now, I would have found it very difficult to sustain such an argument. Ethics do not need the Bible. Academic ethics committees do not consult religious texts, and I am glad they do not. So in the secular world people have already ditched the Bible as a source of authority for ethics as well as science. Yet still Christians in their discussions seem to want to believe that it does have something important to say in ethical matters, perhaps even the final word.

This is impossible to sustain, even taking a cursory glance at some passages from the Bible. For example, let me quote Leviticus 19: 19 'You shall keep my statutes. You shall not let your animals breed with a different kind; you shall not sow your field with two kinds of seed; nor shall you put on a garment made of two different materials.' Should we perhaps picket our local department store demanding that they stop selling polyester/cotton shirts as they are an abomination to the Lord? And should we demand that no farmer ever uses a mule since it is the result of abominable sexual relations between horse and donkey? There are hundreds of these laws.

Much of the ethics in the Bible often no longer make any sense at all. So many passages seem to be odd. This should hardly come as a surprise; many were written for a nomadic people living in a semi-desert in the Middle East some three thousand years ago. Their rules were not wrong, they were their way of ordering their society then. That does not readily translate to our society today. And at times some of the episodes we read about seem to stem from an entirely different morality. We actually see that, in our terms, God and his servants can behave wickedly.

Did God really hate Egyptians so much that he would

slaughter all their eldest sons as described in Exodus? Why does the Bible condemn homosexuality but not paedophilia? In fact at times it even encourages sex with girls as well as ethnic cleansing – don't believe me? Read Numbers chapter 31. Actually Numbers 31 stands out; for here we see Moses in action and it's not a pretty sight. Do we really want to take our morality from a man who ordered the slaughter of every Midianite little boy? Do we want to be told how to live by a man who ordered the killing of every Midianite woman who was not a virgin (Numbers 31:17)? Do we want to take sexual advice from a man who suggested that every virgin could be kept for the soldiers (Numbers 31:18)? This kind of thing makes for uncomfortable reading for those who wish to claim that the Bible is eternally valid.

I realise that some will defend the Bible come what may. I hope it does not appear that I am mocking such people or being hostile towards them. I really don't mind if archaeologists wish to search for the remains of Noah's Ark. And many Bible-believing Christians are good people, with an exemplary morality, which has been fed by their faith. However many of us simply cannot accept such interpretations of the Bible. In certain circumstances these interpretations can lead to great injustice, especially in the treatment of women and minorities. Let us not forget that the Bible was used to justify slavery, apartheid and the subjugation of women, and in Africa is still used to justify the terrible treatment of gay men and lesbians.

For most educated intelligent people what an ancient tribal leader had to say about homosexuality is simply no longer relevant. Most of us have friends who are gay or lesbian; we know that they are not evil. People want love, friendship, companionship and understanding whatever their sexual orientation. What Moses had to say on the subject, or St Paul for that matter, simply doesn't affect the way I consider my gay and lesbian friends. We've moved on. And whenever Christians start quoting the Bible as if it were a divine handbook, more and more people not only disagree but feel positively revolted. It is not that they are simply offended by the opinions of people who treat scripture as if it knew everything about right and wrong, they are put off reading scripture altogether. And that is a tragedy.

A few years ago a friend of mine was planning on getting married. She and her husband-to-be were entirely non-religious, so the wedding itself was to take place at a lawyer's office in the north of Scotland. I was asked if I would be prepared to hold a ceremony of some sort in the hotel afterwards for all the guests. I was honoured and so I devised a kind of ceremony which involved listening to music about love while reading some purple passages, and it ended with the two of them making promises to each other which they had written themselves. I was proud of what I had done. Of all the weddings I have ever conducted this was the most beautiful. All my readings were from non-religious sources except the last, which was from 1 Corinthians 13 in the Bible. Afterwards three people came and asked me where I had got such a wonderful passage. They had never heard it. These were the kind of people who had been put off reading the Bible by what they saw as the intolerance of certain Christians.

I can think of no better definition of love than 1 Corinthians 13 verses 4 – 7: 'Love is patient; love is kind; love is not envious or boastful or arrogant or rude. It does not insist on its own way; it is not irritable or resentful; it does not rejoice in wrongdoing, but rejoices in the truth. It bears all things, believes all things, endures all things.' That is glorious, beautiful and the kind of love I would wish to give and receive. So I can read 1 Corinthians 13 and consider it marvellous because it carries its own authenticity, its words resonate with my experience, that is how I have found love to be at its best.

Yes, the Bible contains stuff about the world that is factually incorrect; yes it contains some horrendous passages; yes it contains rules and opinions with which most people would profoundly disagree. But it also contains in no small measure some of the greatest wisdom and talk of justice that I, for one, know. We must be able to read the Bible as we would any other literature written between 3,000 and 2,000 years ago. To read the Bible in this way does not denigrate it, far from it, by reading it in this way we can really engage with what it has to say.

Many Christians talk about 'a problem passage'. What do they mean? Normally I take it to mean a passage with which we would profoundly disagree were it anywhere else but the Bible. If we are forced to agree with the Bible then it can be very difficult to read at a particular point, the passage itself becomes a problem. If we read the Bible as we would read any other piece of ancient literature then the passages in question are not problems. We can disagree with them. If we do this then actually we might find that the Bible is a much better read than we imagined.

Let me take an example. I currently work with people who have mental health problems. Stories about forgiveness, rules about hospitality, stories about heroes of faith being rejected by authority, these all resonate with people. The Bible has given me a storehouse of stories, rules and myths which have helped me make sense of sometimes extremely traumatic situations.

When I first became a Christian I believed that the Bible had a divine stamp of approval. I remember signing a piece of paper that said that the Bible had 'supreme authority in all matters of faith and conduct'. But I found it a hard read. I have to confess that while I believed in the authority of the Bible I didn't spend a great deal of my private time reading it. Now I find myself often reading it, grappling with it. The reason is not that I believe God somehow gave it to me, but that it actually contains stories and wisdom that still help me make sense of my life.

This attitude to the Bible is absolutely vital if Christianity is ever again to be taken seriously. If the study of the Bible is to have any credibility whatsoever, then it cannot be treated as if it were a sacred text that must not be challenged. Such an attitude might prevail in some Churches, but if it were to do so in the field of academia then theology could not rightly be considered an acceptable discipline, because its study would not have genuine academic rigour. It would be rather like the subject of Physics being dominated by sun-worshippers who refused to analyse light because it was sacred. This is why many universities have theology departments which themselves have departments of biblical studies.

There are extremely positive things that can be said about the books of the Bible. Any educated person can agree that here is a book that contains the distillation of the religious ideas and wisdom of a particular group of people spanning a period of perhaps a thousand years. We can agree that some of the laws suggested in the first five books of the Bible have been so effective that they have influenced legislators ever since. We can agree that the criticism of the leaders of Israel by those known as the prophets contain a very advanced attitude to the poor. We can agree that some of the teachings of Jesus of Nazareth are spellbinding in their implications. All these things are true however we view the source of the authority of the Bible.

The fact is that for reasons we don't fully understand a race of people we now call Jews had an extraordinary vision. Influenced by an Egyptian Prince called Moses, these people, some of them fleeing slaves, had a vision of the divine as a source of justice. They set up a nation that struggled to survive, surrounded by great powers, and many of them did not let go of their vision. For perhaps about two thousand years these people attempted to understand their God and their world. As Christians we must never forget that Jesus and St Paul were both Jewish. The Bible is the sum of the collected wisdom of these people. It is their attempt to make sense of the world and understand God. There is not another book like it. It is a book about the divine; it is not a divine book. Yet in its pages people have had visions of God for thousands of years.

I fear that the decline of Christianity in the west has meant Churches have considered themselves under siege. As a result many have considered that biblical criticism is part of the attack. Even books like this are considered to be anti-Christian, and people like me are often accused of not being Christians. This reaction becomes a self-fulfilling prophecy. The attempt to defend some of the ludicrous parts of the Bible, the attempt to believe that it is all 'true,' actually stop it being read at all.

Such an attitude is incredibly frustrating. This

literalising of Biblical stories takes away their power. Personally I love the story of Adam and Eve, a fascinating insight from the ancient world into human nature that can still make sense. Cain and Abel, as well and Noah and the tower of Babel, all in the first 11 chapters of Genesis, are all great ancient mythological stories; far more accessible to me than, say, Greek or Norse myths. Yet these stories did not happen, they are myths, they were always intended to be myths, their truth is not dependant on being a record of real events but rather being a mythical explanation of human nature.

Likewise, and here I'm treading on more controversial ground, the story of Jesus' birth is also a myth. The stories of Jesus being the son of a virgin, echoing similar contemporary myths, is an attempt by Matthew and Luke to say that Jesus was in some sense divine. John does this in another way by speaking of the eternal word becoming flesh. This is mythical language. It did not happen but for the writers it is   true.

So when we read the Gospels we need to be aware that the earliest of them (Mark) was written about 40 years after the death of Jesus. None of the writers had ever met Jesus, yet his teaching and his authority had been passed on to them. They wanted to put his teaching in written form, and so they used a traditional Jewish method of writing known as Midrash, whereby they reused ideas from the Old Testament to inform their stories. They used mythical language and they used polemic. I will talk a little more about this in the next chapter.

The Bible covers the beginning of the world and its end. Human nature is explored. Heroes are introduced with all their glories and their flaws. It is a book of contradictions and errors, but it is also a book of beauty and truth. I believe that the Bible has something to say to all people regardless of whether or not they consider themselves Christian or Jewish. The Bible profoundly affects those who choose to read it, not because it is holy but simply because in many of the meanings of the word, it is good.

5
JESUS

If the Bible is considered to be the 'word of God', then in one of its books it makes a similar claim for a historical person. In the first chapter of St John's Gospel a man is described as 'the word' or to be exact in this man 'the word became flesh' (John 1:18). The name of the man was Jesus and he came from an obscure Galilean village called Nazareth. Some of the teachings of this Jesus are at the heart of what I want to say in this book. For me, the Christian faith remains what it always was, the teaching and the example of this young Jewish Palestinian peasant. This teaching, this example, remains for me some of the most powerful and effective in the history of the world. I say this not because it's in the Bible but because when a great deal of this material is read it still makes sense. I say this because when I read the accounts of Jesus' life and teaching, especially as they appear in the first three gospels (Matthew, Mark and Luke), I can see that in this material is a worthwhile basis on which to build my life.

A few years ago I was invited by a local newspaper to go and see a production of a new version of the musical

Jesus Christ Superstar by Andrew Lloyd Webber and Tim Rice. I was given two free tickets in return for a written criticism of the production. It was my one venture as a theatre critic. It can't have been that good as I was never asked to do it again. However I remember being very struck at just how much the musical had dated. It had a very '60s' feel to it. Jesus came across as a kind of peace and love hippy. Many versions of the Gospels do this; mystery plays present Jesus as a medieval wonder worker, nineteenth-century versions seem to make him into a Victorian moralist. Yet the Gospels themselves, though clearly set in first century Palestine, have a strange timelessness about them. Jesus of Nazareth comes across as distant and mysterious, yet strangely contemporary and real.

Traditionally Christian doctrine speaks of something called the incarnation. This means that God himself, in some sense, became a human being. Because God is so mysterious, so different, so 'other' he has given us a means to understand him. If we look at Jesus we see God; 'To have seen me is to have seen the father' Jesus is reported to have said in St John's Gospel. St Paul, the first Christian writer, describes Jesus as 'the image of the invisible God'. This then is the traditional Christian answer to the questions human beings have about the meaning of life.

The problem is that many people simply cannot accept that this was true. The idea of a god becoming human seems to be an ancient one, which worked two thousand years ago but no longer resonates. So again the issue becomes belief, if you don't, won't or can't believe that Jesus was God you tend to ignore him. Christians often say that to really appreciate Jesus you have to give your life to him. To most of us that makes no sense at all, so we leave Jesus to those who are into that kind of thing. Yet, if you get behind the myth and the magic, the teaching and life of Jesus of Nazareth still have an immense power regardless of who you think he was.

As a matter of fact a great deal of scholarship has gone into the attempt to unearth the historical character that we read about in the Gospels. Those involved are said to be taking part in something known as the 'Quest for the Historical Jesus,' and intellectually this fascinates me. For many Christians this can seem a strange idea, it is assumed that Matthew, Mark, Luke and John are brief biographies. They are not, they were written many years after the events they talk about and they are written with spin. It is therefore a very important part of scholarship to try and discern a little of the historical character who lies behind the Gospels.

What I witnessed in Jesus Christ Superstar was one take on Jesus, written by two middle class English men at the end of the 1960s. It was their interpretation of what Jesus was on about. The idea of an interpretation of the events of the life of Jesus begins in the Bible. Each gospel writer clearly has a very different take on the man whose teaching inspired 'him' to write. If we read the Gospels in chronological order we can actually see how Jesus changes. He seems to become less human the further the writers get from history. So for Mark, the first writer, Jesus seems to have been born normally and is declared as God's son when he is baptised (Mark 1:11). Ten years later it must have been asked what Jesus was before this baptism, and so we have the story of the virginal conception. This was written probably 80 years after the supposed event in Matthew and Luke. Later still the writer of John's Gospel does not include the story of Jesus' conception but instead says that Jesus was the eternal word existent at the beginning of all time.

So in each Gospel Jesus comes across quite differently, over time he keeps being promoted but equally becomes less and less human. This dehumanising of Jesus seems to have carried on after the canonical gospels were complete. There were many other gospels written after John and in most cases Jesus' miraculous abilities keep growing as his life seems to become less and less rooted in history and more and more the stuff of legend. Personally I do not particularly like his character in John's Gospel; it is the Jesus of Matthew, Mark and Luke who attracts me. For example in Matthew 14:11 Jesus says: "For all who exalt themselves will be humbled, and those who humble themselves will be exalted." By the time we read John's gospel he says in chapter 14 verse 6: "I am the way, the truth and the life no-one comes to the Father except through me". I don't want to sound sacrilegious but this sounds a tad big-headed.

It is at this point that I need to come clean. When I first became interested in Christianity a wise man suggested that I read St Luke's Gospel. I knew surprisingly little about the life of Jesus. What I read of his teaching and life had a profound effect on me. I was eighteen years old. I fell in love. It had all the hallmarks of other experiences of falling in love; sleepless nights, heart palpitations, inability to think about anything else. That was my first experience of such a deep love, and like all first loves it has never really gone away. I have of course fallen in love since; But what I read about Jesus had a lasting effect on me and in part made me what I am. My feelings have altered, there have been ups and downs and things I used to believe about Jesus have changed, but the love itself has remained. It is therefore extremely difficult to write calmly and with academic integrity about this subject. I am biased. But I am not alone; this feeling for Jesus is shared by millions of people all over the world.

It is worth considering what on earth made a working class boy from a non-religious family in north of England have such a reaction to an ancient piece of Jewish literature. And this applies not only me, because to be a Christian at all means in some sense to have a deep love and respect for this remarkable man. But it is also worth remembering that all experiences of love are subjective, we see different things in different people and most experiences of love to a certain extent hold up a mirror to the person with those feelings. The little we see of Jesus we see in the pages of a book, so there is a tendency to fill in the gaps and make him the person we would like him to be. I suspect that George Bush worships a very different Jesus than did Martin Luther King.

I was a very idealistic teenager. I had an early interest in politics and found myself far to the left. I felt very strongly about the iniquities of the modern world. Why was it that some people seemed to have lots of everything while others worked hard and had very little? Why were people discriminated against on the grounds of colour, gender, sexuality or class? I wanted the world to be better, to be fairer. I got involved in left wing politics but became increasingly frustrated by my fellow 'revolutionaries'. They seemed humourless and uncaring. When the revolution came they accepted that some people would suffer, but the ends would justify the means. Almost as if to prove their callousness many socialists in England in the 1970s happily defended the Soviet Union when it was clearly apparent that the regime there was morally bankrupt and economically incompetent.

So I desperately wanted the world to be fairer but had yet to find a body of people who I could join. At this point

I ended up in Israel, having won the annual essay competition of the York Anglo-Israeli Friendship Society (really). It was there that, for the first time, I encountered people for whom religion was a primary motivation in their lives. I even stayed with an Orthodox Jewish family where the man of the household was an Auschwitz survivor. This was a totally unexpected experience; I realised that religion was not merely a fantasy, it did something to people, it changed lives.

It was soon afterwards that I read St Luke's Gospel. Jesus, the main character, seemed to answer many of my questions. He seemed to be seriously against the inequalities of his society, telling rich people to give all their money to the poor. Yet he seemed to care for the individual, and above all he lived what he preached to the point of death. I saw Jesus of Nazareth as a working class man from the north of Israel who spoke to my politics and to my emerging spirituality. As I said, I fell in love.

And then I joined the Church. At first Christian talk of Jesus all made sense. Of course I felt like this about Jesus, I was told, because he was God in human form, it was his purpose to speak to our humanity. I was led to see beyond the teaching about equality, about generosity. I was led to think less of what Jesus said and more about who he was. This was fine, I had fallen in love and I was given an armoury of ways to express that love. I was told the amazing thing about Jesus was not his message, but his very being. The messenger was the message. The most important thing about him was that he had risen from the dead. The second most important thing was that he was the son of a virgin and was therefore divine. Jesus had preached about a possibility called the Kingdom of God. However if I was to be part of the Church I should preach about Jesus rather than the Kingdom.

And that was what I did. I preached Jesus till I was blue in the face. That was what a Christian did, that was mission. Yet over time it ceased to work. For all my talk about self-fulfilment, basically the whole thing seemed to boil down to a simple transaction. God sent Jesus into the world to live a perfect life and to suffer so that my imperfect life could be forgiven and I could go to heaven. I was trying to persuade others to believe the same things, only the more I thought about it the more the whole thing looked like, well, utter and complete nonsense.

It was therefore a great relief to go back to the Bible, back to the Gospels and begin to see that actually that was not really the main part of what Jesus taught at all. Clearly the idea of a sacrificial death is there in the interpretations given by the gospel writers. The idea of a sacrificial death was how St Paul seemed to have interpreted the life of 'Christ Jesus'. Yet in the words attributed to Jesus himself in the first three gospels this idea was minimal. If you have only heard of Jesus through traditional Church teaching that can come as quite a surprise. I can only recommend that you read Matthew, Mark or Luke for yourself.

Think of the teachings of Jesus that we all know well: "It is easier for a camel to go through the eye of a needle than for someone who is rich to enter the kingdom of God" (Mark 10:25). It is interesting how people take the instructions from the book of Leviticus about homosexuality literally yet read this teaching of Jesus metaphorically. Think of the "Prodigal son" (Luke 15:11-32) where the father forgives his son unconditionally and doesn't seem to need a bloody sacrifice in order to do so. Think of the "sheep and the goats" (Matthew 25:31 – 46) where judgement is based on the way we behave towards the poor and has nothing to do with somebody dying for sins. These are the teachings of Jesus.

It is quite remarkable just how little notice is taken of what Jesus actually said. It makes me angry. Sometimes I think that the message Jesus was trying to get across has been hidden by those who claimed to preach it. For example within traditional Christianity, a Christian is often said to be a person who believes the 'Nicene Creed'. This was written in the third century under the Emperor Constantine as a definition of Christianity. It has been used ever since and in many churches is recited every Sunday as part of the worship. This creed says a great deal about Jesus but there is something missing, read it and note well:

We believe in one Lord Jesus Christ,
the only son of God,
eternally begotten of the Father,
God from God, Light from Light,
True God from true God,
Begotten not made,
Of one being with the Father;
Through him all things were made.
For us and for our salvation he came down from heaven,
Was incarnate from the Holy Spirit and the Virgin Mary
and was made man.
(_____)
For our sake he was crucified under Pontius Pilate;
He suffered death and was buried.
On the third day he rose again
In accordance with the scriptures;
He ascended into heaven and is seated at the right
hand of the Father.
He will come again to judge the living and the dead,
And his kingdom will have no end.

Notice where I have put (_____). That is
the point that shows what is missing. For between his
birth and his passion Jesus taught some incredible things.
Not one is mentioned. Nothing is said about loving one's
neighbour, about turning the other cheek, about living in
the moment. By exalting Jesus to God's right hand it seems

as if we can ignore his powerful message, he has become the message himself. Not merely Jesus but primarily his death. Christianity becomes 'Cross-tianity'.

This exalted, mythical, magical Jesus is not the character with whom I fell so inextricably in love. It has taken me many years to recognise this. Of course to a certain extent we will never be able to get back to the historical Jesus. Simply by reading St Mark's Gospel and then looking at Matthew, which was probably written some ten years later, we see dramatic changes to the depiction of Jesus. We can only surmise how many changes took place between his life and the writing of the first Gospel. Be that as it may we have a body of literature that purports to speak to some extent about the life and teaching of Jesus. This body of literature paints a picture of a warm, compassionate man who had a vision of a better world, which he called the Kingdom of God.

Of course in reading the Gospels we are presented with strange phenomenon – miracles. For some people these are proofs that Jesus was a wonder worker. Yet for others these are obstacles to faith. People might believe in the message but stumble over the miracles, the stuff of ancient literature and pre-scientific humanity. We know for example that dead people do not get out of graves and bodily walk about. But neither St Paul nor St Mark depict Jesus as doing anything of the kind; it is only later that Jesus seems to become more miraculous.

One thing is of paramount importance in understanding Jesus. He was a healer. In our days of modern medicine it is hard to imagine what life was like for poor peasants in the Mediterranean 2000 years ago. It was harsh; people lived short, brutish and painful lives. There was nobody to turn to in sickness other than the wandering healers who occasionally passed through a village. Jesus was just such a healer and I suspect he was a particularly effective one. Of course those who witnessed his healings did not report scientifically about what had happened; they interpreted the events as they saw them. If somebody was on the point of death and a religious healer managed to save them; that was understood to be a miracle. I think that is how we must understand so many of these strange stories that come across in the Gospels.

If we examine the healings further, we learn that Jesus did not seem to heal for his own financial gain. Rather he healed with a message, the message of a possibility of new life in something he called the Kingdom of God. This Kingdom was rarely understood to be the place we go when we die, but a present reality, brought about by people having new kinds of relationships. We see this particularly in what Jesus told his disciples to do on their own mission (Mark 6:6-13). He sent them out in pairs to take nothing with them but to accept hospitality when it was offered and to heal. As far as I understand the earliest stories of the Church, this is precisely what happened not only under instruction from Jesus but after he died. The message was so powerful; it could not be destroyed by killing its proponent. The message was so powerful that some 2000 years later and 2000 miles away a young man wanting to change the world was inspired to change his life. It is a message that retains its power today.

And that kingdom remains a powerful metaphor for how we can change our world for the better. We still need to break the powers that destroy societies and individuals, not by violence but by living differently. I don't know precisely how to bring the message of Jesus bang up to date; it's probably not possible. But I believe that Jesus can be an inspiration to many people, whether they believe him to be the incarnate word of God or just an inspired man.

It is probably the case that many readers of this book have never actually read a gospel. If I could do one thing I would suggest you do just that. Pick up St Luke's Gospel, recognise that it was written years after the death of Jesus, that it explains some of his actions in ways that we would not. Recognise also that parts of it are probably historically inaccurate, at some points you may disagree with Jesus and that many of the things that are said about him are spin. Take all that and read the Gospel of St Luke and hear its message. I sincerely believe that if more people were to do just that, it might make a difference.

I wish to finish, not with a creed but with some words of Jesus hinting at a way of life which seems so relevant, even here thousands of miles away, thousands of years away. They are all from Luke's Gospel:

'Friend your sins are forgiven'(5:20), 'It is not the healthy who need a doctor, but the sick. I have not come to call the righteous, but sinners to repentance' (5:31-32), 'Blessed are you who are poor, for yours is the kingdom of God' (6:20), 'Love your enemies, do good to those who hate you' (6:27), 'those who are least among you all – they are the greatest'(9:48), 'Ask and it will be given to you, seek and you will find, knock and the door will be opened to you' (11:10), 'Do not be afraid' ((12:6), 'Who of you by worrying can add a single hour to your life? Since you cannot do this very little thing, why do you worry about the rest? (12:25-26), 'Sell your possessions and give to the poor' (12:33), 'From everyone who has given been much, much will be demanded' (12:48) 'Everyone who exalts themselves will be humbled, and those who humble themselves will be exalted' (14:11), 'When you give a banquet, invite the poor, the crippled, the lame, the blind, and you will be blessed' (14:14), 'You cannot serve both God and money' (16:13), 'Let the little children come to me and do not hinder them, for the kingdom of God belongs to such as these. I tell you the truth, anyone who will not receive the kingdom of God like a little child will never enter it' (18:16-17), 'It is easier for a camel to pass through the eye of a needle than for a rich man to enter the kingdom of God' (18:25)

These sayings are just some of Jesus' pithy ideas. I find writing them out that I am struck by how far such an attitude seems from the belief system imposed by the creed. Jesus demanded a change in lifestyle; the creed demands a change in belief. It is only the former that can change the world.

6

WORSHIP

Traditional Christianity argues that God speaks to us in the Bible and through the life and message of Jesus. But alongside that there is a requirement made of Christians that they attend worship, in order to praise and to listen to God. I have even heard it argued that it is only when worshipping that people are fully human. While prayer is seen as a conversation, in worship God is present. The biblical line is often quoted: 'Where two or three are gathered there shall I be.'

Prayer is not unlike smoking – almost everybody has tried it at least once. Worship on the other hand has not been tried by everybody. Perhaps in Western Europe the majority of people under 40 have never really engaged in worship apart from weddings, funerals and the odd carol service. For all that, worship is actually a lot easier than private prayer. Worship comes in different shapes and sizes and can be designed around most personality types. Whereas I have always struggled with private prayer, I have been moved to the depths of my being in corporate worship. Even now whenever I sing the words 'Intercessor, friend of sinners, earth's redeemer, plead for me' from the hymn Alleluia sing to Jesus I get a tingle down my spine. Intellectually I'm not sure I agree with the ideas, emotionally I am moved by the sentiment.

Worship does not only refer to God. People worship other people and have a deep psychological need to do so. Go to any sports ground on a Saturday afternoon, to any pop concert and even a book signing and see people worshipping. A quick scan of the twentieth century shows the variety of ways people have worshipped other people, from Albert Einstein to Hitler to Elvis. Certain people attract adoration from others who would do anything for them. As a young boy I worshipped Peter Lorimer, a footballer with Leeds United and Scotland; as an adolescent I worshipped John Lennon of the Beatles and as a grown man I find myself, like many others worshipping Nelson Mandela. Of all living people, were I to meet him I would go weak at the knee. Worship does not have to involve screaming, singing or waving hands in the air. Worship of this kind seems to involve the belief that another person is superior to ones self and in some way or another deserves adulation.

If this kind of feeling about other people comes naturally then it is easy to understand how worship of God follows. In 1973 at the age of ten I had a serious falling out with a friend who was a Leeds United fanatic; to irritate him I supported Sunderland against Leeds in the FA Cup final of that year. I could no longer worship Peter Lorimer. I stopped worshipping John Lennon when I began to think other bands might be as good as the Beatles. Anyway nowadays the media helps us realise that all our heroes have flaws, nobody is perfect. Therefore if we can postulate a being who is perfect or remember a historical figure without a fault then our worship will not disappoint. This I think in part explains the insistence in Christian circles that Jesus was as we are, yet without sin. He was perfect, and no grubby journalist is going to prove otherwise.

Human worship of people varies enormously. Teenage girls worship the singers in boy bands in a different way to how teenage boys worship sports stars. Likewise intellectuals worship their mentors differently to how poets worship their muses. So when we think of worship of the divine we should not be surprised at its variety.

My problem with Christian worship is not the idea; people need to worship. You only have to look at the worship of a demagogue like Hitler to see how dangerous non-religious worship can be. On the whole therefore the worship of a first century Jewish pacifist with, in my opinion, some of the greatest insights in history is unlikely to be harmful. And on the whole most Christians who worship are not a wicked bunch of people. My problem with worship is simply how utterly banal, boring or ludicrous most of it has become.

Please forgive me if what follows is a caricature, but I hope it makes the point. And anyway I always rather enjoy caricatures. As I have implied throughout this book, I have been around the Christian circuit. On the whole my experience of worship began with the banal, moved into the ludicrous, and inasmuch as it is anywhere now it has settled with the mind-numbingly boring.

Banal worship is what I have experienced in charismatic and evangelical circles. This kind of worship frightens a lot of people. Yet if you analyse what is going on, it is limited to telling God or Jesus just how wonderful they are. And the more earnestly you say this, the more the worship is considered good. In this kind of worship people often experience ecstatic moments where they feel themselves to be completely given over to God. With eyes closed, hands waving in the air and a simple melody being sung, this can feel the most wonderful of all experiences, almost orgasmic.

Yet this worship is empty. It says nothing, it achieves nothing. Two things happen; God is told that he is wonderful and the worshipper can, for a moment, feel very close to God. Yet people who experience this kind of worship do not seem to be better people than others. If this kind of worship really did put a person in intimate relationship with an infinitely merciful and loving God one would expect enormous amounts of mercy, justice and love to come from the churches where such worship happens. But

I cannot name one person of this type as a modern day saint of the order of Ghandi, Martin Luther King or Mother Theresa. It is spiritual masturbation. It leaves the person concerned feeling briefly relieved, but it produces nothing.

I wonder what such worship does for God. Does he really need to be told how wonderful he is? This is a serious question. Why on earth (or in heaven for that matter) does God need me to spend hours singing his praises? Does he not realise that he's wonderful? Can God be insecure, needing millions of people to build up his confidence?

Consider a fairly well known modern English hymn. If you are unfamiliar with modern hymns, they basically dwell on telling God how great he is. This is fairly typical:

Majesty, worship His majesty,
Unto Jesus be glory, honour and praise.
Majesty, kingdom authority,
Flow from His throne unto His own,
His anthem raise.
So exalt, lift up on high the name of Jesus,
Magnify, come glorify Christ Jesus the King.
Majesty, worship His majesty,
Jesus who died, now glorified,
King of all kings.

If this hymn matters to you, please forgive me. I don't

really believe that singing this through three times with your eyes closed and your hands in the air does a great deal of harm. But does Jesus need it? If he requires us to sing such stuff it seems odd coming from somebody who apparently said 'Those who exalt themselves will be humbled'.

For a while I found such hymns to be deeply moving. I found that I could sing them with almost every atom of my being. All that I was wanted to give Jesus the power due to him. I wanted Jesus to be the Lord of my life and while I was singing such hymns this seemed to be possible. At times anything seemed possible. However whenever I contemplated the consequences of this kind of worship it was minimal – in fact virtually nothing beyond giving my money to the Church and feeling guilty about the fact that I wanted to (and later did) sleep with my girlfriend.

The world was not a better place because I got off on these hymns. God was no more or less wonderful because I loudly proclaimed that he was and I was not a different person. Nothing changed. The whole thing was banal.

Yet I could not let go of my desire to be close to God. I was dissatisfied but not in despair, so I moved to a different type of worship. This was worship I found in traditional Anglo-Catholic churches, though it will be seen in many other places. Essentially this worship works by being serious and mysterious. Churches are brooded over by statues, stained glass and icons. Worship is accompanied by ancient music, strange sounds and the exotic smell of incense. If I'm honest this is still the worship I enjoy the most. But it is ludicrous.

Whereas banal worship emphasises the nearness of God, ludicrous worship emphasises the distance. In this, God is a mysterious, unapproachable being whose presence is mediated by another authority, the Church. Usually this kind of worship is sacramental. The theology that lies behind it is both silly and positively dangerous. While God is unapproachable, those given authority by the Church can make him present. Therefore, for reasons I have never fully grasped, the priest is able to turn bread and wine into the body and blood of Christ, give a divine blessing and even forgive sins.

It is worth just thinking about what I have written. When certain people do certain things, and the more mysterious they make these things the better, they can make God present. They are able to control God. What is more God won't turn up at the bidding of a lay Christian or one not ordained by a Bishop. Strange that God doesn't prevent war, won't answer the prayer of the dying but turns up whenever a priest calls, like an obedient dog. Not that the bread actually looks like anybody's flesh, but apparently it is. The Emperor's new clothes spring to mind.

As a result priests have been given amazing status and authority. A priest can give you God's forgiveness; a priest can get you into heaven. And so for years priests have been treated with utmost respect, while it turns out that some of them have been abusing this respect in the most shameful ways.

This kind of worship, by appearing to be otherworldly, gives the impression that it speaks of the mystery at the heart of the universe. It is simply just mysterious. Orthodox Christians see their worship as a taste of heaven. Somehow by joining their worship you are seeing, hearing and smelling eternity. If it helps so be it, mystery can have that effect. It works equally well in Hindu worship and in a great deal of new-age stuff.

The Roman Catholic Church seems to be caught between ludicrous and banal worship. It has kept the idea that its priests can deliver God on demand, despite the horror of what many of them have done to children. At the same time in many places it has got rid of the images, the bells and the smells and is beginning to sing banal hymns and even has charismatic worship. And of course, as children see long before adults, most of its worship is simply boring.

For myself I recognise the psychological effects of both the above types of worship. I used to enjoy the experience of imagining that God was within me or that a priest could deliver him to me, only I stopped believing it. The result was that I still wanted to worship, but I couldn't get too emotional or mysterious, so my style of worship was devoid of either. This is what Anglicans call 'middle of the road.' The only problem is that such worship is tedious. Christians arguing about the exact wording of the Eucharistic prayer is preposterous. Most people listening to a priest droning over the same words week in week out are not analysing the words that he or (occasionally) she says, they are mentally writing a shopping list!

And so worship is an odd spectacle. Sunday by Sunday the same group of people come together and sit in long lines facing an empty table and a strangely dressed individual. They repeat the same words punctuated by different hymns. They listen to texts from the Bible, most of which they do not remember by the end of the service, and they are preached at. Usually this is the result of habit. Once you've been doing it for years it's hard to stop. For others, church is an experience that came with childhood, perhaps they left years before, but aging or tragedy have brought them back. But for most people of my acquaintance the idea of going to church doesn't enter their heads, even when thinking about the meaning of life.

So for the majority worship is a tedious waste of time. For years I encouraged families who were non-churchgoers but whose children were to be baptised, and couples preparing for marriage, to come along. For years they came when I asked them to and stopped as soon as they could. I can count on the fingers of one hand the number who became regular church members as a result. The problem was not that they felt any animosity towards the Church;

just simply that it said nothing to them. It bored them.

Clearly there is a massive decline in church-going. All three types of worship are less popular than they were. Church leaders find this hard to stomach and want churches to be relevant and entertaining, but still people do not come. But despite all this people long to worship. That is the irony of the whole thing.

I think the problem is the dissonance between hope and realisation. Or put more simply, Churches are not scratching where people are itching. There is clearly a longing to connect with our inner selves, to search for meaning in the universe. Human beings have a spirituality that will not go away and longs to be engaged. Yet the Churches do not meet these needs.

Occasionally, after several beers, friends of mine confess that they do think about the meaning of life. They want to connect with God. Yet turning up at any church simply does nothing for them. In my present work I see an increasing interest in Eastern religions especially Buddhism and New Age spirituality. This comes at the expense of Christian worship. I suspect that at the heart of the problem is the insistence that worship is tied to belief. For example I know people who really have enjoyed bouncy charismatic worship and been horrified to discover that most of the people who take part believe that a practicing homosexual is going to hell. Likewise people simply refuse to believe that individuals can forgive sins or turn bread and wine into the body and blood of Christ. The large majority simply does not accept that God has given the Church to be his presence on earth. Or that He has given us the Bible as His word.

This really is the sticking point. Educated people do not believe that anybody, any book or any institution, contains all that is necessary to understand what life is about. To become a full member of any Church seems to require a public statement of belief that most people simply cannot make. If you have ever had to say the Nicene Creed in the middle of a service you might know what I mean; many people tell me that they do so with their fingers metaphorically crossed. Apparently, if you cannot accept this creed you are not a Christian. Well in that case, reply an increasing number of people, 'I can't be a Christian'.

And so we come back to the same place we have found ourselves throughout this book, the issue of belief. In reality, what has worship to do with belief? The desire to be in touch with God seems to be a gut reaction of many human beings. To bend the knee to something outside of myself is something I have to do. To acknowledge something greater than I can see, hear or feel puts this 'something' at the centre of my world. There is something I cannot understand which helps me to believe that I am not the centre of the universe; there is more to life than can be explained. I am happy to call this something 'God' though

I realise others will give it, or him, or her, another name. Worship is my attempt to stop being at the centre of my own life and put this 'God' there.

Lots of people tell me that they would love to go to church. I believe them, I think the idea of worship is almost hard-wired into humanity, it has existed in all cultures and as far as we know in all periods in history. Why is it for example that even in times of desperate poverty vast amounts of money, time and effort have been put into temples, stone circles, churches or whatever? This effort serves little evolutionary purpose, but we need it. And when people actually point their innermost beings away from themselves and towards a God, there can come a sense that their very selves are fulfilled. I do not believe that for all our sophistication we have lost our desire to worship. We need however to find ways of expressing this urge which are intellectually satisfying.

But so much worship at present concentrates on God. I am increasingly uncomfortable about defining God. I do not know what God is (see Chapter 2) and I will not allow my worship to be dictated to by what other people tell me about God either.

Am I alone? Surely there must be others who would wish to seek to worship what we do not understand. Yet this will take creativity, it will demand recognition that 'the Church,' if the word has meaning, is those people who attempt such worship, and not an institution that imposes it. Worship will surely involve people who wish to find God in themselves and in their community and not those who believe they have already found God, have defined 'him' and wish to defend their definition. Worship may also involve people coming from many traditions and faiths, all accepting that many paths lead to the truth.

This chapter ends with a personal plea. I am not a touchy feely type of person. For me the worst part of any Christian worship is 'the Peace' when we're suddenly expected to turn to a complete stranger and shake them by the hand, or give 'friends' a hug. I do not like holding strangers by the hand, or closing my eyes and appearing to be in ecstasy. But I do enjoy communal singing. I wish to engage my brain and refuse to leave it outside. I am also a man and enjoy the company of other men as well as women, yet in most churches women outnumber men considerably. Surely there must be a form of Christian worship that could engage my brain and my heart, which acknowledges my search for 'God' but also acknowledges that any definition of God is inadequate. What will I and others like me do?

Too many Christians have reached this point and given up. I will not do that. I am convinced that there are thousands of people who wish both to search for God and to do so together. We should not abandon Christianity to the fundamentalists who believe they know what God is like and how 'he' should be worshipped.

At the heart of the idea of worship is an acknowledgement that there is something greater than self and putting self into the hands of that something. We live in a world where self-worship and self-promotion are not only acceptable but expected. Yet people feel empty and unfulfilled. We live in a world where people have all they want and yet still sense that there is something missing. We live in a world where most people claim to believe in God. In this world many of us have a need to reach out and connect.

It is almost too difficult to name what it is we want to connect with – it can appear to be deep within us and it can feel to be strangely beyond us. Words like 'love', 'truth', 'meaning' 'absolute' all point to it but don't manage to encapsulate it. For some the all-encapsulating word is 'God', for others that word is itself the problem. Whatever the word, whatever our understanding, many of us long to try and connect. That surely is the essence of worship. That surely has a lasting value. Worship therefore must not simply be what people who believe certain things do when they get together – but rather an expression of our deepest yearnings.

PART III

WHAT ABOUT LIFE?

Even a purely moral act that has no hope of any
immediate and visible political effect can gradually
and indirectly, over time, gain in political significance.
Vaclav Havel

There is no such thing as the State
And no-one exists alone;
Hunger allows no choice
To the citizen or the police;
We must love one another or die.
W.H. Auden

7

MORALITY

You may think that the most compelling argument in favour of religion is ethics. Religion in all its forms, it is argued, gives us a sense of right and wrong. I have many times heard it argued that things like the Ten Commandments give us our rules to live by, without them there would be moral anarchy and general chaos. Furthermore if people can be persuaded that breaking moral rules can actually lead to eternal punishment it has a sobering effect upon their actions – sometimes literally considering the number of teetotal Christians.

With the ending of the apparent moral certainty associated with religion has come a change in general morality. We do not live as the Victorians did, especially when it comes to sex and marriage. There is a fear around that there is simply no anchor upon which to base ethics. I remember once as a vicar catching a boy who had stolen some money from a collection plate. I chased him for what seemed like an eternity and finally cornered him. He handed back the money. When I asked him why he had stolen it he said it was because he needed it. 'But don't you see it's wrong?' I asked. His reply took me by surprise. 'It's only the law that says it's wrong – the money will make me happy and not keep you lot miserable'. I was so impressed I let him go.

What that young boy demonstrated was moral relativism. The fear is that without some kind of base we will make up the rules as we go along. For centuries religion seems to have given us that base, that anchor, and we fear that if we lose it we are in trouble. In the western world with the decline of religion it can seem as if we're entering a terrifying experiment. I suspect that never before in history have so many people believed that there is no moral absolute. As this belief continues to grow it creates a kind of panic that we do not quite understand. That is surely why for example there is so much respect for the Roman Catholic Church, it almost doesn't matter what they believe; at least they believe something. Furthermore it is this fear of moral relativism that often brings people to church in the first place. People with children remember how their morality was formed by the Church and they wish the same for their own children.

The desire for moral certainty can be fulfilled by a belief in a straightforward God. The traditional Christian view of God includes that of law-maker. Many chapters of the Bible contain very straightforward rules as to how we should live. If we follow them then we are acting as the universe wishes us to act. We know where we are, we have Moral Absolutes!

This thinking is extremely persuasive but is perhaps not quite as convincing as it at first appears. Most evidence suggests that religious people are not more moral, not better than anyone else. Just think about the religious people you know. They might not swear very often but are they better people than others? In my experience they are generally not – that's why they are so often accused of hypocrisy. Personally I rarely wear my dog collar because among other things it makes people think that I'm a 'Good Person'. I'm not! Really. In fact writing a chapter of a book on the subject of morality makes me feel nervous. I have a sense of right and wrong, sometimes in line with traditional Christian teaching and sometimes in opposition to it. I am also aware of my own failings and the fact that there are many people who are far moral than me. What am I doing writing about morality? I suppose my answer is that unless we leave morality only to those who are perfect, we who are flawed will have to do the job.

There are some exceptionally good people in this world and exceptionally bad. I have a sneaking suspicion that most people under duress will do some pretty wicked things, and under other circumstances can be quite saintly. Whether they are religious seems not to make much difference. I trained for a ministry in a theological college that contained about sixty people. You might have thought sixty people training to be vicars would be a place of good morals. It was the bitchiest place I have ever been and to my knowledge every imaginable sin, with the possible exception of murder and rape, happened while I was there. So let's put the idea that Christian people are good firmly out of our minds.

The fact of the matter is that most morality comes to us through self-interest. I do not hit you when you annoy me because I do not wish you to hit me when I annoy you. I am honest so that you will be honest. It's not rocket science. The great Scottish enlightenment philosopher, David Hume, reckoned that all human moral action could be explained as deriving from a mixture of self-interest and sympathy. Hume saw that as well as self-interest, people seem to have an ability to enter into another person's distress, and in so doing also seem to have a wish to alleviate it.

But where do we get the rules? Within traditional Christian thinking a good starting place is the Ten Commandments. For many people these ten rules are thought to be the basis of all our ethics. So below you will see the Ten Commandments as they appear in Exodus 20: 1-17. But don't read them yet. If they are so vital – do you know what they are? Can you remember them? If you can't, don't worry. Not even a random sample of six of my clergy friends could remember all ten:

1. I am the Lord your God…you shall have no other gods before me.

2. You shall not make for yourself an idol, whether in the form of anything that is in heaven above, or that is on the earth beneath, or that is in the water under the earth. You shall not bow down to them or worship them.

3. You shall not make wrongful use of the name of the Lord your God.

4. Remember the Sabbath day and keep it holy. Six days you shall labour and do all your work. But the seventh day is a Sabbath to the Lord your God; you shall not do any work.

5. Honour your father and mother.

6. You shall not murder.

7. You shall not commit adultery.

8. You shall not steal.

9. You shall not bear false witness against your neighbour.

10. You shall not covet your neighbour's house; you shall not covet your neighbour's wife, or male or female slave, or ox, or donkey, or anything that belongs to your neighbour.

Are they really the ten best moral rules that have ever been thought of? I don't think of myself as completely wicked, but I'll be honest with you, I have broken over half of the above and I break two of them pretty regularly without even feeling guilty (I'll let you imagine which ones).

These are not eternal rules. Consider for example number ten. In that one sentence we see part of the problem. First of all it implies that a person can own a slave. Now I don't know about you but I consider that doing so is far worse than, for example, screaming 'Oh my God!' when I hit my thumb with a hammer (number three). Secondly, consider commandment ten's view of women. You are not to covet a belonging of your neighbour's and these belongings seem to be listed in order of value, house, wife, male slave, female slave, ox and donkey. So in this commandment a wife is a piece of property. We no longer think like that. Our morality has moved on.

Most people I know would consider murder always wrong; adultery, stealing and lying to be usually wrong, and jealousy to be unprofitable. However even murder can be justified in self-defence or mitigated by circumstance. For an abandoned spouse, who is not technically divorced, having sex would not be considered wrong by most. Stealing to feed a starving family could even be right, and we can all think of white lies that should have been told. Circumstance and situation change the way we behave. Most of the simple rules can be worked out by considering how people might best live and work together in society. Sadly not everything is simple.

The fact of the matter is that we live complicated lives in a complicated world and we do not have a handbook to get us through the ethical dilemmas we all face. As far as we can see Adolf Hitler was a loving uncle, a caring vegetarian and a constant friend. Uncle Joe Stalin was a loving family man while F. D. Roosevelt as we now know was an adulterous cheat. Roosevelt may well have personally been more of a failure in the Ten Commandments department than the other two. Yet few of us would deny that Roosevelt was the better man.

So religion, and Christianity specifically, do not give us our ethical rules. These tend to be worked out by society in order for society itself to function and its members to flourish. If religion has had an impact it has been to reinforce society's rules by giving them divine sanction.

In one particular area Christianity seems to have actually been harmful, and that is in its sexual ethics. How many Victorian teenage boys' lives must have been made a misery by being told that masturbation is the one unforgivable sin? Many people were only liberated from guilt on this subject by Alfred Kinsey. Likewise homosexuals, women with a high sex drive, those who have had children out of wedlock, those who are divorced have all, at different times been made to feel that they are unworthy. Indeed many Christians to this day have vaguely uncomfortable thoughts about sex, that its pleasure is somehow sinful, that it is a little dirty. I comfort myself with the words of Woody Allen, who said that sex is only dirty if you do it right.

For many of us who call ourselves Christian it is this area that fills us with the most embarrassment. I still recall telling people that sex outside marriage was wrong while sleeping with my girlfriend. I still cringe when I hear that the Roman Catholic Church hierarchy, made up entirely of elderly male celibates, tells women what they can and can't do with their bodies. I hang my head in shame when I hear my own Anglican Church condemning practising homosexuals when my own experience is that the proportion of homosexuals (practising) is far higher among priests than any other group I know. And when it comes to a body of celibate priests abusing children my anger runs over. When it comes to sex, Christians seem to be hypocritical to the core.

Taking all of the above, it would be quite logical to argue that religion has no value at all in our ethics. And to a certain extent that is true. As I said in Chapter 4 a book like the Bible is not a document of eternal ethical value. When it comes to making rules, self-interest and sympathy seem sensible enough ideas. In fact Jeremy Bentham's notion of Utilitarianism seems to work well for our lawgivers – the greatest happiness of the greatest number.

Yet I have a sense that there is something missing. Self-interest and utilitarianism can explain why we behave morally; they can give us precepts for law. Religious rules per se seem as relative as any other. Yet most of us have a gut reaction, at the very centre of our being, that certain actions are simply right and others are wrong. I'm not only here talking about conscience, which Freud explained as the superego, that part of us which keeps our childhood sense of guilt alive. I have a core belief that there is something divine to morality.

One of the things that people seem to admire the most is self-sacrifice. Avoiding murder, being honest, just, kind and generous can all be explained by self-interest. Yet some people take this a step further. There have been those throughout history who have sacrificed their lives in one way or another for the greater good. And it is these we most admire. That, in fact, is the story of the cross. It is the story of those who have died for a greater cause. There are countless numbers who have given up money or family or pleasures for the sake of God or others. These kinds of sacrifice go beyond those that can be explained by self-interest. They also go beyond those that can be explained by religious imperative. There are simply human beings who are prepared to give of themselves totally. And it is these who we consider the most moral – even if they break certain rules.

Occasionally in any community there are those people who everybody seems to love and respect. I have at times been privileged to take the funeral of such a person. Even if I have never met this individual it can be become quickly apparent that they were special. Almost invariably when I ask about these people I am told that there was 'something about them'. Usually I also discover that they seemed to be around when others had their tragedies, that they were the ones who knew what to say, they were the ones who discreetly helped people out financially when nobody else knew. These are the people who make us realise what goodness is. Yet they go beyond rules. The Ten Commandments do not lead to such behaviour, nor does utilitarianism. And we know that, and hence we say that there is 'something' about somebody.

What is that 'something'? Time and again throughout this book we have come across that moment when we are lost for words. It is as if we reach a point perhaps with an individual, perhaps with a thought, perhaps with a situation when words will not suffice. It is the same with morality. For often at a funeral discussion, when a good person dies I am told 'they wouldn't have hurt anyone'. That is ordinary goodness, couched in negative terms, what somebody wouldn't have done. Yet we seem to have a sense that there can be more. Those whom we think of as best are those whose lives seem to be lived as a gift. The traditional term for this is Grace. The idea that God gives totally is seen as Grace. And those whose lives seem to mirror this may offer Grace too.

Those who live in this way may be Christian, they may

belong to another religion, they may hold no creed. I hope they will forgive me if I say that in them I see something of God.

Basic human ethics, the rules by which we live, can be calculated and worked out in any given situation. Trying to derive them from the Bible, or from Church teaching is confusing and ultimately self-defeating. I am not saying anything new. Throughout history Christians have recognised this. It is what St Paul called justification by faith, whereby the keeping of rules simply does not achieve anything. It inspired the Reformers like Martin Luther to turn away from the heavy burdens of religious obligations. Yet time and again people return to the idea that there are and there can be eternal rules to live by – that God is the eternal lawgiver.

In one of the most moving sermons ever reported, Matthew tells us that Jesus went up a mountain to teach (Matthew Chapters 5, 6 and 7). For Matthew this is a deliberate imitation of Moses receiving the Ten Commandments on Mount Sinai. At first it seems that Jesus is giving us a new series of rules to live by. What follows is far from that, and is known as the Sermon on the Mount. On the whole, this sermon sets out an ideal that few if any can live up to, yet which those who 'have something about them' often seem to come close to. There is a shorter version of this in the second half of Luke 6.

I put the Ten Commandments earlier in this chapter. I wish to say a few words about this sermon. If you read the sermon you see quickly that like Moses, Jesus sets up rules. However the rules are far stricter than those of Moses. For example concerning murder; Jesus says that a person is culpable even if they simply get angry. Lust is seen as the equivalent to adultery. You should not merely love your neighbour but love your enemy. When I read all that I can confidently say that I am an adulterous murderer incapable of love. And that is the point – we can't do it. Trying to live by statutory rules is self-defeating, and makes those who try feel guilty and inadequate. By pointing out that we are all inadequate we see the human ethical dilemma.

Towards the end of the sermon Jesus comes out with the golden rule; 'do to others as you would have them do to you' (Matthew 7:12). Though Jesus did not coin the phrase that surely is the essence of his ethics. He also commands us not to judge others. Our ethics need to be worked out for ourselves. Jesus seems to be aware of moral relativity. Furthermore he accepts it as a reality, he recognises that his society has moved on from the nomadic tribe under Moses. We should recognise that we have moved on from first-century Palestine.

For me the genius of this teaching is that it begins with a tradition, the teaching of Moses. It critiques that teaching by emphasising its impossibility and suggests therefore an entirely new way of accessing morality by working it out for ourselves. Surely we can do the same. We can take the

Christian tradition, not set it in stone, but use it to work out morality for ourselves.

Another problem with using the Bible as a moral standard is that it says nothing about nuclear war, global warming, abortion or a whole host of ethical dilemmas we face in the twenty first century. However using templates like 'do to others as you would have them do to you' gives us the kind of basis on which to build a morality.

Morality and ethics affect all of humanity; they are not the preserve of the religious. However if we wish to live lives that are noted for their generosity, self-giving love and goodness beyond simply sticking to the rules then there are aspects of religion that can help. For at the heart of Christianity is the myth of absolute self-giving, the idea of a God who gives of himself, of a man whose life seems to have been wasted by a pointless self-sacrifice and the imperative of the followers of that man to do the same. And ultimately Christianity claims that such lives have far more value than those marked by success, power or wealth.

We know all this. Think of the best, the most moral person you know, not the irritating person who is a prude and who never swears. Rather, think of that person who you know could be trusted with your life. Think of that person who never condemns yet makes you a better person. What are they like? How would you like to be like them? If that person has a faith, what is it in? How does it make them like they are? What would the world be like if we were all like that?

8
GENEROSITY

I said in the last chapter that if we extend the notion of morality we come to the idea of self-giving, of lives filled with Grace. We sometimes look at people and wonder how they can be so generous and how they also seem to remain so happy. For me, Christianity at its very best can lead us on to such a way of living. In many ways it is this element of Christianity that keeps me within the Christian fold. So much of the search for meaning, of the search for God, is a self-indulgent attempt to be content with one's own life. But this aspect of Christianity, concerned with generosity, seems to take the whole thing much further.

At the heart of Jesus' teaching was a rejection of the poverty of so many people around him, and a horror at the wealth of the few. Doubtless Jesus grew up seeing immense suffering, which could have been avoided for just a few coins. Perhaps it was this that led to his famous, or perhaps infamous, comment that: 'It is easier for a camel to pass through the eye of a needle than for a rich man to enter the kingdom of God'. Perhaps it was this that inspired his followers to hold everything in common and to 'sell their possessions and goods and distribute the proceeds to all, as any had need' (Acts 2:44-45).

I want therefore in this chapter to consider the notion of generosity. I believe that one of the greatest legacies that Christianity has given us is that of giving. It is worth noting for example that hospitals began in Christian Europe with the monasteries. Look at the number of charities which were started by Churches or individuals inspired by their faith. Many of these charities remain Christian to this day. And many of the others are still staffed by Christians. Many Christians see the giving of money and time as the essence of their faith.

However like so much else, the duty to give has been exploited. I remember as a young student, new to the faith, being told of the importance of tithing. To tithe is an Old Testament concept whereby 10% of one's income was to be given to the Temple in Jerusalem. This was taken by certain Christians as being translatable to the Church. Therefore I understood that it was my duty to give at least 10% of my student income to the Church. This income I may add was given to me by my parents in order to enable me to be educated. I gave this money to the Church willingly, and this particular Church was highly successful employing a large staff and keeping its building in good order.

Now just put these two ideas together. At first we have

Jesus' notion of the unfairness of his society. We have his followers giving their incomes to the poor, but we have translated this to me giving my money to the Church. How many desperately poor villages on the southern fringes of Europe have ornate and expensive churches? How many people in Africa give of their meagreness to vast and relatively rich congregations? I'm trying not to be cynical here, but it does look as if somebody somewhere is being exploited.

As a matter of fact in Old Testament times it was probably the Temple that saw to the distribution of money to the poor. The prophets constantly remind the religious leaders of their duty to the widow and orphan above the rituals of worship. Widows and orphans were the poorest people of all in that society, unable to survive without an adult male income. Certainly in the west the Church was the main source of support for the poor until the instigation of the welfare state. So until that time, to give to the Church was, to a certain extent, to give to the poor. I was once vicar of a medieval English parish church that had at the back a large wooden wall-mounted box that was known as a 'dole cupboard'. This was so called because from it bread would have been doled out to the unemployed on a weekly basis. This is why English people often call unemployment benefit 'the dole'. That helped me to see how the state took over the duties of the Church in supporting the poor. Therefore in a sense our taxes play the same role as the tithe used to.

But the Churches use this notion of tithe to create their own wealth. In North America for example the result can be enormously wealthy Churches. Likewise, although not using a tithe, the Roman Catholic and Orthodox Churches seem ornate and inordinately wealthy while in England, although it pleads poverty, the Church of England remains the country's third largest landowner. All of this has come about from the accumulation of wealth collected from people who have been led to believe that supporting the Church is in some sense giving their money to God.

And supporting the Church is not necessarily a bad thing. Churches still, as I said above, are leaders in charitable work. Often it is Churches that attempt to work with young people, with drug addicts and homeless people, helping them escape poverty and prostitution. Furthermore the Churches have recently been at the forefront of campaigns against Third World debt. Nevertheless we are all aware that this is not enough.

We know that actually the unfairness of the world that Jesus witnessed is as real today as it was then. There are still millions of people who die needless, painful deaths for the lack of a few coins. There are children in some parts of the world who are taken to camps and taught to return to their villages and murder their parents, there are millions of women selling their bodies and risking AIDS in order just to feed their children. The fact is that the people of

North America and Western Europe can ignore such poverty if they wish. Cleverly, we have virtually abolished absolute poverty where we live and to a certain extent we have done so by exploiting those we cannot see. We rape the earth all over the world for cheap commodities. We are aware that some of our goods are so affordable because people are being paid barely enough for a bowl of rice a day. Yet we live with ourselves because we don't have to look at it, we don't have to face it. And when occasionally the death toll becomes unbearable we might send a few dollars or buy a pop record and hope that the pain goes off our television screens.

Somehow when I think about the poverty of the Third World I am almost sick when I hear that a Church is collecting money to buy a new set of intricate vestments or to support a new evangelist who will bring new people into a congregation. Surely this is not what Jesus meant when a rich young man approached him and asked what he might do to achieve eternal life. In Mark 10 the story goes like this: Jesus first tells him to keep the last six of the Ten Commandments (interesting), which he gets slightly wrong (so if you didn't know them all – you're in good company). He then tells the rich young man to sell all he owns and give it to the poor, then follow him. Notice Jesus does not tell the man to give his possessions to the Temple, or to Jesus himself, but to the poor. That is the point.

Throughout the synoptic gospels to give to God is to

give to the poor. The story that Jesus tells in Matthew 25 about the final judgement is very instructive. It is the story of the last judgement when the 'Son of Man' will divide the nations as a shepherd divides the sheep from the goats. In this story it seems better to be sheep than a goat. Goats always seem to get a raw deal in the Bible, though personally I prefer them to sheep. Anyway, the judgement seems to be based on how people responded to those in need. The sheep are told they will inherit the kingdom for 'I was hungry and you gave me food, I was thirsty and you gave me something to drink, I was a stranger and you welcomed me, I was naked and you gave me clothing, I was sick and you took care of me, I was in prison and you visited me' (Matthew 25: 35-36). When the Son of Man is asked how this can be they are told that 'just as you did it to the least of these who are members of my family, you did it to me' (Matthew 25:40). Likewise the goats are rejected because they failed to respond to this need.

This is compelling stuff. It kind of makes sense at that deep level I keep returning to. Surely, those who give of themselves to the most needy are those who are nearest to God. This seems to be one of Jesus' most insistent points. Yet so many Christians seem to ignore it. There is even a theological movement called the 'prosperity gospel' that argues that your own personal wealth is a sign of just how far God has blessed you. In his marvellous book The Protestant Work Ethic and the Spirit of Capitalism, written in 1905, Max Weber argues that Calvinism said that certain people were the elect of God, predestined to eternal life. However you could never be sure if you were one of the elect. But if God blessed you with the ability to work hard and rewarded you with material benefits then that was a sign that you were. This kind of thinking seems to have influenced many Protestant countries, perhaps most notably the US. But it all seems a long way from a humble carpenter telling his followers they had to sell their possessions and give to the poor.

In most western countries the amount of money people give to those less fortunate than themselves is woeful. I am writing these words yet I am ashamed at my lack of generosity. In the end I know that I should give, but my selfish desires, not only for life's necessities but clothes, holidays, alcohol and all the rest stop me from helping as much as I ought.

But there are those who do give. We only have to watch the news and learn of charity workers giving their time, their money and even their lives for the sake of others. In many shanty towns will be found humble friars, missionaries, or secular charity workers who have given up their lives that others may have a better chance. Where would the world be without these people?

Even in the western world there are certain areas that are seen as 'no-go'. Estates where murder is common, poverty is rife, where prostitutes walk the streets and crack cocaine is sold openly on street corners. In these areas illiteracy rates are high, petty crime can be intolerable. Social workers, health workers, police and other professionals come in and do the best they can. However to this day there can be one type of professional who still lives in such places, among the people, among the petty crime. The priest, perhaps Anglican, perhaps Roman Catholic, is prepared to share his or her life with people who all other professionals will only visit. Usually the priests in these areas are single as those with families will not move there. Most of these priests are gay. Yet we see in these people a level of self-giving that Christians can be proud of. Likewise Salvation Army Officers live and work among those who nobody else would consider sharing their lives with. This is the generosity that makes me believe that there is something to following this God that is still worthwhile.

Of course reading about monks, nuns and Salvation Army Officers also offers a cop out. Both demand a level of self-giving which is beyond most of us. Perhaps sex and families, money and alcohol are things we could not live without. However they are put forward as an extreme and as a possibility. At the heart of Christianity, at the heart of the message of Jesus of Nazareth, was an idea of living generously for the sake not of self, but of 'the other,' both God and stranger. As a matter of fact one of the things that we are learning alleviates depression is self-giving.

Voluntary work for example often gives more to the volunteer than to those they are seeking to help.

And now at the beginning of the twenty first century we have never needed such sacrificial living so badly. For years westerners have sought more and more material goods. Suddenly most of us find ourselves wealthier than our grandparents could ever have imagined. When I think of my own grandmother bringing up her seven children what she might have given to have the things I have is unimaginable. As a fairly low paid hospital employee with three children I am still able to own a home, a car, an automatic washing machine, a dishwasher, TV, video, DVD player and so on. At least once a month I eat in a restaurant, I holiday at least twice a year, often in hot climes. The list is endless. Yet I am aware my insatiable desire to consume, to travel, to rest, might not only be making me selfish but might also be destroying the planet. The world itself needs me to live generously, to live frugally, to sacrifice my own selfish desires for the sake of 'the other'.

It is in this that once more we can see God speaking through. Of course the idea of giving money to an institution is not good enough. Of course translating the message to share with the poor into putting money on a collection plate is probably wicked. However let us not lose that idea which underlies such thoughts. The idea that we have generously received and we must generously give in return.

I guess like many people the one thing that has been both the hardest and the most rewarding in my entire life has been the job of being a parent. Nevertheless, having children teaches us at a profound level the meaning of altruism. I remember the shock of my eldest daughter's first Christmas; I was more interested in her pleasure than my own. Throughout their childhoods I have wanted more for them than for myself. I'm not saying I haven't at times resented the effort, time and money they have used up. I'm not saying there aren't times when I have read the paper rather than listen to their demands. However like most parents they have taught me a level of loving, generosity and compassion that I would never otherwise have understood.

But the job of being a parent is universal. Indeed I recently bought a puppy and his own canine mother seemed to show a similar self-denying altruism that I experienced. It can all be explained genetically, caring for my children protects my genes; it is selfish. And when we see how much effort parents give to getting their children into better schools than other children we see just how selfish it is.

The notion of true giving therefore must extend beyond our own families. That is at heart the positive side of the celibate life, where someone denies themselves a family in order to devote themselves to a more general self-sacrifice. It also explains what many people find one of the most puzzling teachings of Jesus. Let me quote from Mark 3:31-35: 'Then Jesus' mother and his brothers came; and standing outside, they sent to him and called him. A crowd was sitting around him; and they said to him, "Your mother and your brothers and sisters are outside, asking for you." And he replied, "Who are my mother and my brothers?" And looking at those who sat around him, he said, "Here are my mother and my brothers! Whoever does the will of God is my brother and sister and mother."'

This passage has been woefully misused by certain Christian groups to take people away from their parents. However, in the context of a life led generously this demand is clear. If we are to change the world we must see others in the same way we see our families. Human history has shown the gradual realisation of our responsibility to others. You can see how family ties turn to tribal ties, that turn to clan ties, that turn to national ties. People give their taxes for the poor in their own country and their lives to defend it. But to take it one step further, perhaps now we should look at humanity as we look at our own families. I try and imagine the kind of person I might be if I really saw a hungry African child in the same way as I see my own daughter. It is almost impossible to imagine, yet some people seem to take that leap. If more did the world might be truly turned upside down.

9
THE CHURCH

This book has attempted to look at some of the most important themes in Christianity. There has been an enormous temptation to dwell on the negative, to consider the ways that good ideas have been distorted. I hope therefore that I have also suggested positive ways forward. One of my greatest desires is that people can be honest about their doubts and their struggles. Many years ago I concluded that the greatest threat to faith is certainty. Yet certainty is what so much of distorted Christianity seems to offer. Interestingly the certainty differs. Christians are often very certain; they simply differ about what it is they are certain about! For example the two sides in the religious divide of Northern Ireland are both Christian and they seem pretty certain that they are right. Sadly that kind of certainty seems to lead to bigotry and violence.

My own faith is a doubtful and questioning faith: I know people who wonder whether it is even a Christian faith. I cannot help it, I am even confident that most of the things I believe with conviction will one day be considered wrong by people like me. In fact I know that in years to come I will reread this book and be amazed that I could have said some of the things contained here. Nevertheless in this chapter I wish to express my feelings of despair when I think of the Church. But I also wish to put forward a vision and a challenge of what Christians meeting together could achieve.

Most Christians believe in something rather strange, a nebulous concept called 'The Church'. By 'Church' I do not mean the building in the High Street but rather the people who meet in that and other buildings. If you are a Roman Catholic this is easy; the Church is an institution created by Jesus, passed on to St Peter and the apostles and still in existence today. You are aware that there are other Christians, but basically for all their good intentions and deep faith they are not actually part of the complete Church. For Protestant Christians the Church is more problematic, for it is not an institution as such but rather a spiritual community to which all true Christians belong and to which the various institutions and denominations bear witness.

All of the above is in the realm of theology. I doubt it enters the consciousness of most Christians. Whether you are a Roman Catholic or a Protestant you might have read all that and thought 'But that's not what I believe'. And that I think is part of the problem. Belonging to most Churches (and there are notable exceptions) seems to involve having to believe certain things. As I said in Chapter 6, many people attend worship because they wish in some sense to be close to God; what they find is that they are told what God is like. Belonging to a Church seems to mean gathering with people who share your beliefs. If those beliefs are not shared in their entirety then people tend to keep quiet.

Yet for many years I have been very honest about my doubts, my questions, and have been amazed at the positive response I have received, often from staunch members of the Church. For example I remember preaching that I hadn't got a clue what happened to people when they died but that I rather suspected that death was the end. At first I was subjected to an angry rant from a lady for whom belief in an afterlife was axiomatic. However she was followed by a series of people who said they had rather thought the same but had been afraid to mention it. I have talked of my disbelief in the literal virgin birth and resurrection and have been amazed to discover that committed Christians have thought the same for years and imagined sadly that they were alone. In fact the only people who seem to get angry about these beliefs are the clergy, the guardians of correct belief, known as orthodoxy.

The problem for the Churches is that tying their existence to belief systems seems to create more problems than it solves. So many people today simply never consider entering a church because they do not think they believe what they are meant to believe. I have had many frustrating conversations, often with adolescent boys who do not believe Adam and Eve were real people. It is no use telling them that I don't believe that either; they have concluded that Christians believe bollocks and therefore that Christianity is bollocks.

It's not only awkward youngsters who create these questions; it is responsible, well-read intelligent adults too. My guess is that if you have got this far into this book, you perhaps feel a little like I do. If that is so, you may feel a similar despair to me. Why are there no Churches speaking this language? Where can a person go who has profound spiritual questions but does not believe that there are simple answers? Why are Churches so mind-numbingly boring? I could spend pages detailing the problems I see with the Church, but I do not wish to do that; instead I would like to share a vision and offer a challenge.

As always I want to go back to Jesus. Today perhaps the most significant moment in Jesus' short life is seen as a meal, the so-called last supper that Churches remember regularly, sometimes even daily. This recollection is usually called the Mass, the Eucharist or Holy Communion. It recalls Jesus' last meal before his arrest and subsequent execution. However if you read the Gospels you might note that this meal was the last of many. Jesus seemed to spend an enormous amount of time eating with people. At the wedding in Cana of Galilee, with 5,000 people on a hillside, at the home of Simon the Pharisee, at the home of Zaccheus the Tax Collector, after his resurrection on the road to Emmaus and by the Sea of Galilee. When he sent his disciples on their mission he told them to heal and then to eat with those they had healed. When the early Christians met they ate and drank together to such an extent that St Paul worried that some were getting drunk. Moreover Jesus had such a reputation for eating with people that he became known as a glutton and a drunkard.

Now I find this idea of eating with people instructive. On the whole we eat with people when we are close to them. We eat with our families; we eat with our close friends. Relationships move into a new stage when people eat together. Often a first date is a meal; two work colleagues signal that they want to work more closely by having lunch together; we eat together at weddings and funerals. Loneliness can feel very real when a person consistently eats alone.

For myself there can be nothing better than gathering with a few friends over a meal, a few beers and a good laugh. When we eat together we come together as a community. One of the great problems of our day is that families do not eat together. I think that in getting people to eat communally, beyond the ties of tribe and family, Jesus signalled a new type of relationship. He was criticised for eating with publicans and prostitutes because even if you have to speak to such people you should not eat with them. Later his followers created further scandal by encouraging Jews and Gentiles to eat together.

And somehow in the Churches this radical sharing of food and lives has been translated to nibbling on something that looks suspiciously like a biscuit and sipping a tiny amount of wine. The whole thrust of the message seems to have been subsumed into a vaguely magical ceremony where incantations are said over bread and wine and they become something else, the body and blood of Jesus. This pseudo cannibalism seems such a long way from the wandering carpenter talking about a Kingdom that would turn the world on its head. Why not start by eating together?

Instead of getting ourselves worked up about what we believe and whether that is the same as what somebody else believes, surely we should simply start eating together and listening to one another. A great many Churches have already discovered this; the Alpha course for instance gets people together for a supper where they feel relaxed. Sadly this is followed by a talk presenting a very narrow version of Christianity. That is not my vision.

I have a dream of living closer to other human beings than I do at present. At one time I imagined being a monk, in fact there were only three things that stopped me, the poverty, the chastity and the obedience. Likewise I have always had a hankering to join a commune but I'm too attached to my material comforts. But what I wouldn't give to be part of a group of people who all felt themselves to be on the search for God and meaning who met regularly to share their thoughts, to work for justice and to eat together. We often look at cliques of people with a mixture of annoyance and envy. We are annoyed that a group of people do not wish to be open to others and jealous that we are not part of such a close group. What I dream of is a group of people truly open to each other and welcoming of newcomers.

What would such a community look like? Well I can only imagine what it might do for somebody like me. I began this book discussing how hard I find prayer, but nevertheless benefit from sitting quietly. I would love to be open about this with others and find out what happens to them when they try to pray. I would love to share ideas and listen to experiences over a meal. The struggle to be in contact with God, ultimate reality or whatever you wish to call it is fairly universal, yet most of us are embarrassed to talk about it. In a truly open Christian community surely this would be the backbone of what people wished to do.

I've talked about God. I've tried to emphasise how difficult I find other people's definitions of God and any attempt I make to define God is equally problematic. Yet I do not want to let the idea of God go. There is something within me, at a deeper level than my mind or my emotions that seems to resonate with the idea of 'something' else. I have had many conversations, short and fleeting, with others who feel the same. Let us be open to each other and meet and talk about our thoughts, even when we fear that others will consider them weird.

Likewise I long to understand if my life has a purpose. I would love to get help in finding that meaning and expressing it. I would love to share my confidence about certain things and my insecurities about others. Would it not be wonderful to share some time with people genuinely being open about the deepest yearnings of our hearts?

I talked in the second part about how the Bible and Jesus point beyond themselves to a mystery we call God. I have a deep sense of this God but feel that almost all doctrinal explanations of God fall woefully short. I would love to eat and talk with people who would accept my struggles and not laugh at me because I'm interested in the God questions nor condemn me because I have answered them wrongly. I fervently believe I am not alone and long to share a little of my life with those who think along similar lines. Such a community of people would not have set beliefs but would be open to all attempts at reaching out to ultimate reality.

I've talked about worship; well what better context for humans who long together to be in contact with God than round a meal table together. The Bible suggests that it was while eating together that people experienced worship. I would hope that in this context we could learn what we wanted to do in worship, be open to suggestions, ready to forego some of our desires for the sake of others and all try and discern something of the quiet voice that had led us to meet together in the first place.

Finally in this section I have talked about morality, generosity and justice. I would love to eat with people who took morality seriously but did not condemn those whose morality was different from their own. I would seek a body of people who accepted those who had failed but longed to get it right, a body of people who were not obsessed with sex and accepted those whose home arrangements were not 'normal'. And I would love to sit and eat with people who wanted to make justice real and were serious about making the world a better place.

Beyond that, I simply cannot let the idea of God pass. Not simply as something to talk about but as something at the very core of our being. In our secular world there are those who would love to treat the notion of God as the infantile delusions of a more primitive time. Yet the notion that there is something beyond ourselves, something at the heart of the universe and at the centre of our being, will not go away. God, it seems, cannot easily be shaken off. God is the itch in our soul that longs to be scratched. A lot of this book has been negative about the traditional understandings of God, and for that I make no apology. Yet

I believe in this God to whom great people like Jesus have pointed. I want to try and be in touch with this God and I believe there are thousands like me who feel the same.

And whatever this God might be, this God makes demands. The demands are not easy. They are not about what you believe but about transforming this world into something better. The demands mean somehow using one's talents not for self-satisfaction or self-glorification but for others. This God nibbles at our souls and tells us that we are not doing our best, that we are deluding ourselves if we think that our small contribution is really making a difference. Mainly we ignore this God or pretend our religious observance pleases him or her. A genuine Christian community might just push its members further by reminding them of the demands, and even hearing some new ones.

The book began with a quote from Einstein. We aren't intelligent enough to grasp what God might be, and attempts to describe or codify Him are simply offering false solutions. Let us rest in our sense of God and try to do something about it rather than think in the right way.

Is it all a pipe dream? Often when I listen to people with these kind of views I long to get together. Why is it so difficult? Such a gathering of people would be a Church for me. It would be a Church based not on doctrines but on hopes, it would have no barriers of race, creed, sexuality, disability, or poverty, all would be welcome to gather to eat and if some could not afford to they would be all the more welcome. There would be no barriers of intelligence. Those whose intellectual capacity found more profound thoughts difficult would be welcomed and taken seriously. There would be no barriers of age. Little old women would be as welcome as virile young men; children would be welcome on their own terms. Oh yes, and I know it will be a group with problems, gossip, backbiting, power games and the rest. I'm cynical enough to doubt that it could ever work, but surely it's worth a try.

This could be read as the words of a lonely man who never gets invited to dinner parties! But this is not about seeking friends to make myself feel better. It would not necessarily be a group of friends and differences would have to be worked through.

Such a community of people would be committed not so much to self-fulfilment, though that would play a part, as to the search for truth and the fight for justice.

As a matter of fact the evidence is that the early Church was not a million miles from this - people from all backgrounds coming together to share food and meet each other and God. And this Church had its problems, splits, arguments, incest, laziness and all the rest. But it was this Church that grew phenomenally in the first few centuries of the current era. Surely I am not asking a great deal to suggest that there may well be people who would like to take the risk again. There must be lonely people longing to eat with others, to create a sustainable community of spiritually minded people who are dedicated to sharing some of their time and some of their food for the sake of the search for meaning and the fight for justice.

The fact of the matter is that the Church as we know it in the west is dying. Christians will point to highly successful Churches in Africa, Asia and South America and argue that the future of Christianity lies there. But the growth of Christianity in the Third World probably has more to do with rapid urbanisation than anything else. Victorian England saw a similar phenomenon when huge numbers of agricultural workers came to towns seeking work. These people had no anchor, no sense of place, and found in Churches a place of refuge. After several generations they stopped going to church. Something similar seems to have happened in South East Asia, and will I suspect happen elsewhere.

Certainly in Britain I see an ecclesiastical demographic time bomb. I like old people and I believe they should be a full part of the church; however in most churches I go to they are the only part. I am 42 years old and yet normally the youngest person in a congregation, other than somebody's grandchild who has reluctantly been brought along to give the Sunday School teacher something to do. This cannot go on forever. At the same time there is more interest in religion and spirituality than ever before. The Churches, with their insistence that they have a true knowledge of God simply seem to have nothing to offer people searching for meaning, for ultimate reality, for God.

Most Churches argue that they have some special access to or knowledge of God. Some believe that they can interpret God's word (the Bible) to help us know how to live. Others believe that they can actually and objectively make God present by saying special words over bread and wine. Still others believe that God's spirit can make them do extraordinary things and have extraordinary experiences. If that is so, if ultimate reality can be present in some way in a church, why, many people ask are churches so boring and Christians so bigoted? Surely the God who made roses, tigers and me could do better with those he inspires.

Yet through it all, I still believe that the message of Jesus is worth keeping. It remains one of the most inspiring messages in the history of the world. I still believe that the key themes that are at the heart of Christianity are valuable and can help us all to make more sense of our lives and help us to make the world a better place. Those of us who wish to take this further need to start getting together, start eating together and start making the changes necessary to help augur in the Kingdom of God.

And who knows, God might be with us. In fact maybe we'll see that God has been with us all along but that until we started to listen to each other we didn't recognise what he or she was trying to say

One

Is it getting better or do you feel the same
Will it make it easier on you now you got someone to
	blame
You say...
One love, one life
When it's one need in the night
One love, we get to share it
Leaves you baby if you don't care for it

Did I disappoint you or leave a bad taste in your mouth?
You act like you never had love and you want me to go
	without
Well it's...

Too late tonight
To drag the past out into the light
We're one, but we're not the same
We get to carry each other, carry each other
One...
Have you come here for forgiveness
Have you come to raise the dead
Have you come here to play Jesus
To the lepers in your head

Did I ask too much, more than a lot
You gave me nothing, now it's all I got
We're one but we're not the same
Well we hurt each other
Then we do it again
You say
Love is a temple
Love a higher law
Love is a temple
Love the higher law
You ask me to enter but then you make me crawl
And I can't be holding on to what you got
When all you got is hurt
One love, one blood, one life
You got to do what you should
One life with each other
Sisters, brothers
One life but we're not the same
We get to carry each other, carry each other

One...life

One

Lyrics by U2

O

is a symbol of the world,
of oneness and unity. O Books
explores the many paths of wholeness
and spiritual understanding which
different traditions have developed down
the ages. It aims to bring this knowledge
in accessible form, to a general readership,
providing practical spirituality to today's seekers.

For the full list of over 200 titles covering:

- CHILDREN'S PRAYER, NOVELTY AND GIFT BOOKS
- CHILDREN'S CHRISTIAN AND SPIRITUALITY
- CHRISTMAS AND EASTER
- RELIGION/PHILOSOPHY
- SCHOOL TITLES
- ANGELS/CHANNELLING
- HEALING/MEDITATION
- SELF-HELP/RELATIONSHIPS
- ASTROLOGY/NUMEROLOGY
- SPIRITUAL ENQUIRY
- CHRISTIANITY, EVANGELICAL
  AND LIBERAL/RADICAL
- CURRENT AFFAIRS
- HISTORY/BIOGRAPHY
- INSPIRATIONAL/DEVOTIONAL
- WORLD RELIGIONS/INTERFAITH
- BIOGRAPHY AND FICTION
- BIBLE AND REFERENCE
- SCIENCE/PSYCHOLOGY

Please visit our website,
www.O-books.net

SOME RECENT O BOOKS

Good As New

A radical re-telling of the Christian Scriptures
JOHN HENSON

This radical new translation conveys the early Christian scriptures in the idiom of today. It is "inclusive," following the principles which Jesus adopted in relation to his culture. It is women, gay and sinner friendly. It follows principles of cultural and contextual translation. It also returns to the selection of books that modern scholarship now agrees were held in most esteem by the early Church.

A presentation of extraordinary power.
ROWAN WILLIAMS, ARCHBISHOP OF CANTERBURY

I can't rate this version of the Christian scriptures highly enough. It is amazingly fresh, imaginative, engaging and bold.
ADRIAN THATCHER, PROFESSOR OF APPLIED THEOLOGY, COLLEGE OF ST MARK AND ST JOHN, PLYMOUTH

I found this a literally shocking read. It made me think, it made me laugh, it made me cry, it made me angry and it made me joyful. It made me feel like an early Christian hearing these texts for the first time.
ELIZABETH STUART, PROFESSOR OF CHRISTIAN THEOLOGY, KING ALFRED'S COLLEGE, WINCHESTER

It spoke to me with a powerful relevancy that challenged me to re-think all the things that I have been taught.
TONY CAMPOLO, PROFESSOR EMERITUS OF SOCIOLOGY, EASTERN UNIVERSITY

With an extraordinary vigour and immediacy, Good As New *constantly challenges, surprises and delights you. Over and over again you feel like you're reading about Jesus for the first time.* Ship of Fools *John Henson,* a retired evangelical Baptist minister, has co-ordinated this translation over the last 12 years on behalf of *ONE for Christian Exploration*, a network of radical Christians and over twenty organisations in the UK

1-903816-74-2
£19.99 $29.95 hb
1-90504711-8
£11.99 $19.95 pb

Is There An Afterlife?

DAVID FONTANA

The question whether or not we survive physical death has occupied the minds of men and women since the dawn of recorded history. The spiritual traditions of both West and East have taught that death is not the end, but modern science generally dismisses such teachings.

The fruit of a lifetime's research and experience by a world expert in the field, *Is There An Afterlife?* presents the most complete survey to date of the evidence, both historical and contemporary, for survival of physical death. It looks at the question of what survives-personality, memory, emotions and body image-in particular exploring the question of consciousness as primary to and not dependent on matter in the light of recent brain research and quantum physics. It discusses the possible nature of the afterlife, the common threads in Western and Eastern traditions, the common features of "many levels," group souls and reincarnation.

As well a providing the broadest overview of the question, giving due weight to the claims both of science and religion, *Is There An Afterlife?* brings it into personal perspective. It asks how we should live in this life as if death is not the end, and suggests how we should change our behaviour accordingly.

David Fontana is a Fellow of the British Psychological Society (BPS), Founder Chair of the BPS Transpersonal Psychology Section, Past President and current Vice President of the Society for Psychical Research, and Chair of the SPR Survival Research Committee. He is Distinguished Visiting Fellow at Cardiff University, and Professor of Transpersonal Psychology at Liverpool John Moores University. His many books on spiritual themes have been translated into 25 languages.

1 903816 90 4
£11.99/$16.95

Psalm

PETER OWEN-JONES

The lyrics of the Psalms have survived, being spoken and sung all over the world, because they still communicate the presence of God in all things. Within them are the seeds of understanding, of longing and of being, of being afraid, of being stilled, of being in a state of wonder. But, for many, their language doesn't resonate with contemporary feeling. Once you undo the layers of history and language that have since accumulated you can recover this state of being. Taking its inspiration from rap and country and western this book recasts twelve Psalms in contemporary lyrical genre.

Peter Owen-Jones has been an Anglican priest for ten years and runs four parishes outside Cambridge, England. He is the author of *A Bed of Nails* and *Small Boat, Big Sea*. He recently presented *The Battle for Britain's Soul* on BBC, and his new BBC series comes out in February.

1 903816 91 2
£4.99/$8.95

The Trouble With God

Building the Republic of Heaven
DAVID BOULTON

Millions of people living in the so-called "Christian West" long for a thoroughly modern, intellectually defensible, emotionally satisfying faith which will be unashamedly religious and spiritual in its commitment, but frankly secular in its relevance to this world and this age. Of such is the republic of heaven.

A wonderful repository of religious understanding and a liberal theologian's delight.
MODERN BELIEVING

Written with clarity and sensitivity, The Trouble With God *will make sense to a lot of people who might describe themselves as lapsed atheists, doubtful about Christian doctrine but believing that there must be more to life than a purely materialist journey concerned solely with survival, sufficiency and self-aggrandisement. I recommend it to all.*
TONY BENN, FORMER CABINET MINISTER

The great thing about this book is that it is exactly like its author: it is affectionate, sane, learned and extremely funny. The next best thing to taking David Boulton home for the weekend is to buy it.
RICHARD HOLLOWAY, FORMER BISHOP OF EDINBURGH

David Boulton is a highly entertaining writer, with a great gift of being funny and serious at once. You'll love it!
DON CUPITT, FELLOW, EMMANUEL COLLEGE, CAMBRIDGE

David Boulton's new book fascinatingly shows how a radical perspective on religion can bring together the religious and the humanist...An engaged and cogent expression of the human/divine vision in modern thought.
DAVID HART, WESTAR FELLOW

Disarmingly honest and beautifully written...spurring us on to new visions of the future.
LLOYD GEERING, AUTHOR OF *TOMORROW'S GOD*

David Boulton, humanist and Quaker, is a former TV producer, writes for many religious and humanist publications, and is a member of the British Government's Broadcasting Standard's Commission.

1 905047 06 1
£11.99 $24.95

Bringing God Back to Earth

JOHN HUNT

Religion is an essential part of our humanity. We all follow some form of religion, in the original meaning of the word. But organised religion establishes definitions, boundaries and hierarchies which the founders would be amazed by. If we could recover the original teachings and live by them, we could change ourselves and the world for the better. We could bring God back to earth.

"The best modern religious book I have read. A masterwork."
ROBERT VAN DE WEYER, AUTHOR OF *A WORLD RELIGIONS BIBLE*

"Answers all the questions you ever wanted to ask about God and some you never even thought of."
RICHARD HOLLOWAY, FORMER PRIMUS EPISCOPUS AND AUTHOR OF *DOUBTS AND LOVES*

John Hunt runs a publishing company of which **O Books** is an imprint.

1-903816-81-5
£9.99 $14.95

The Censored Messiah

PETER CRESSWELL

Peter Cresswell has a revolutionary new theory about the life of Jesus and the origins of Christianity. It is a thrilling story, based on modern scholarship, of how a Jewish man tried to change the direction of the religious leadership of his people. It describes a breathtaking piece of brinkmanship carried out against the Roman occupiers of Israel, a journey into the mouth of death and beyond which appeared to succeed.

Peter Cresswell is a freelance writer with degrees from Cambridge and York Universities in Social Anthropology.

1 903816 67 X
£9.99 $14.95

Tomorrow's Christian

ADRIAN B. SMITH

What are the sources of true Christianity? Tradition or Scripture? Experience? How far should our interpretation accommodate modern knowledge?
    Some take refuge in fundamentalism, others in emotion, many are leaving the Church. But there are others, called here "tomorrow's Christian", who struggle to bring together in a meaningful way traditional Christianity and a contemporary, nourishing understanding and expression of it.
    36 short chapters sum up the characteristics of tomorrow's Christian. One who is questioning, ecologically aware, global, evolving, non-theistic, balanced, right-brain, scriptural, prophetic, peace-making, forgiving, empowered, Jesus-following, seeking, free, discerning, post-modernist, meditating, mystical and others. Ideal for discussion groups, and all individuals looking outside their churches for a way to live as Christians.

An inspiring and multi-faceted vision of "tomorrow's Christian." The layout with many short chapters makes the book easy to read and digest. I enjoyed reading this book immensely. I find it stimulating and encouraging.
PHILIP SHEPPARD, *CHRISTIANS AWAKENING TO A NEW AWARENESS*

Adrian B. Smith was ordained as a Roman Catholic priest in 1955.

1 903816 97 1
£9.99/$15.95

Christianity in 10 minutes

BRIAN MOUNTFORD
The best short guide to serious Christianity you will find

You want to know about Christianity? Maybe you've visited a church or cathedral or looked at religious paintings in an art gallery and wondered what the meaning is behind them, why they evoke some sense of mystery and wonder. This short, but profound, "ten minute guide" will help begin to unfold that mystery. Starting with the gospel story, it moves on to the intuitive response to God, the desire for meaning, and how the story can change your life. It answers for the modern reader the lawyer's question to Jesus; "What must I do to inherit eternal life?"

Subjects covered: What is Christianity? Does it work? Can it make you a happier person? Is the Bible true? Do you have to believe in miracles? Do you need to go to Church?

If you want to begin at the beginning with the Christian faith, I can't think of a better way than by sitting down and reading this little book through. Plain-spoken, straightforward, succinct, here is a fresh introduction to the essentials-what Christians believe, how and why they believe what they do, what difference it can all make. If you've been around churches all your life and never fully grasped what it's all about, this is a superb refresher. If Christian faith is brand new to you, what a helpful first step you're holding in your hands.
REV. DR. SAM LLOYD, DEAN OF THE NATIONAL CATHEDRAL, WASHINGTON DC

The most valuable 10 minutes you will spend this year. Gospel truth. The essence of Christianity, simply and memorably explained. Read it.
PETER BENNETT-JONES, CHAIR OF COMIC RELIEF

Could not have been published at a more propitious time in world temporal and religious affairs. Canon Mountford sets forth the essentials of Christian truth that transcend reality. In doing so he aids the preachers whose adherence to inerrancy does more to diminish than to fortify and reinforce it.
ALEXANDER KERN, PROFESSOR OF THEOLOGY, UNIVERSITY OF ILLINOIS

Canon Brian Mountford is Vicar of the University Church in Oxford, one of the most visited churches in England.

1 905047 09 6
$8.95 £6.99

The Thoughtful Guide to Faith

TONY WINDROSS

This book is for anyone who would like to take faith seriously but finds their intelligence getting in the way. It outlines, in 37 short chapters, many of the objections raised to formal Christian religion, and suggests ways of dealing with them which do not compromise people's intellectual integrity.
The claim made here is that Christianity is far more about the way we live than the way we think, that faith can work for all of us, and that what we may or may not believe must never be allowed to get in the way of faith.

"A *bombe surprise*, unexpectedly lively, adventurous and radical."
DON CUPITT, EMMANUEL COLLEGE, CAMBRIDGE

Tony Windross is an Anglican minister in Norfolk, England, with degrees from Cambridge University.

1-903816-68-8
£9.99 $14.95

The Thoughtful Guide to the Bible

ROY ROBINSON

Most Christians are unaware of the revolution in how the Bible may be understood that has taken place over the last two hundred years. This book seeks to share the fruits of the Biblical revolution in an easily accessible manner. It seeks to inform you of its main features and to encourage you to do your own thinking and come to your own conclusions.

Roy Robinson is a United Reformed Church minister, now retired and living in England. A former missionary in Zaire this work arises from a lifetime of study and Bible teaching at the Oxted Christian Centre, which he founded.

1-903816-75-0
£14.99 $19.95